RIGHT & WRONG

CULTURE &

DISCOVERY

Right & Wrong

A Philosophical Dialogue between Father and Son

Paul Weiss and Jonathan Weiss

Basic Books, Inc., Publishers

NEW YORK — LONDON

Second Printing

© *1967 by Paul Weiss and Jonathan Weiss*
Library of Congress Catalog Card Number: 67–28506
Manufactured in the United States of America
Designed by Kay Eaglin

TO JOHN SPEICHER
who gave us the idea

Preface

This dialogue is concerned with basic questions dealing with the meaning of life which have troubled men since the dawn of thought. The participants come from radically different backgrounds and yet have much in common. Paul Weiss is a professor of philosophy. Originally trained in logic, he has become increasingly concerned with the formulation of a systematic world view and the philosophy behind such diverse enterprises as art, religion, politics, history, and sport. Jonathan Weiss, his son, is a lawyer. Interested in literature, he has pursued the law as a means for increasing justice for the poor. The father is primarily concerned with underlying causes; the son, more interested in justifying and explaining the end results. Over the years, we have debated, discussed, and dealt with many issues. Recently, the crucial and basic areas of disagreement and agreement appeared to have crystallized. As a consequence, we decided to see what could be learned from a frank and probing dialogue in which each of us sought to understand and learn from the other. The main concern of this book is the range and interaction of human action and ethics. Each chapter focuses its concern on different aspects of obligation. As a result, certain themes stalk the pages of this volume. It may be of help to identify the nature, relationship, and dimension of the contexts of obligation and to locate certain central questions which reappear in the course of the dialectical inquiry of the book.

The scope of this book is perpetually expansive. The dialectic starts with an examination of ethical obligations of the individual, particularly a young person in school. The inquiry moves to the family, its nature as a unit, its demands and limits. The participants then explore the difference politics and culture make to people, the nature of society, culture, and, finally, mankind. The inquiry which started on the simple level of what an individual's responses should be as an individual has moved to the area of what mankind creates as an ethical obligation and how we all, as members of mankind, owe different degrees of obligation to one another. The final two chapters explore the categories that underlie the whole— what the universe has to do with men and their duties to themselves, one another, society, and the world, and the principles of law and justice that should prevail, both theoretical and practical.

Throughout the discussion theoretical and practical issues appear, reappear, and, we hope, reach some resolution. The first idea concerns why anyone owes something to anybody. The second idea deals with one's role in relation to society and its representatives. The third major question relates to why and how people should be related and obligated to one another. All these issues interrelate and suggest many problems and many concrete questions. Among the practical issues that arise are: rebellion and law; the rights of an individual; the duty to sacrifice. The result is an interchange, suggested resolutions of some basic questions, and perhaps progress toward understanding.

P. W. / J. W.

September 1967

Contents

RIGHT & WRONG

1

The Person
and His Obligations

This first discussion deals mainly with the individual and some of his ethical obligations, particularly in relation to authorities and the factors relevant to obedience. It begins with an examination of the problem of cheating and its bearing on one's relationship to one's classmates. This is followed by a discussion of legal obligations, of the value of athletics, the right and wrong of rebellion, and the moral and educational value of political participation. The discussion ends with a consideration of the problem of young people and their obligations to their society and their contemporaries.

Paul Weiss puts some stress on the rights of authorities and the conditions to which the young are subject. Jonathan Weiss instead emphasizes the experimental character of a genuine education. They agree that there is an objective right and wrong.

JONATHAN: Let's begin with a very elementary question that any-body who has gone to school must have confronted at some time or other. Suppose you are sitting next to another student during an exam and you see that student cheating. Should you turn him in?

PAUL: Does the school have an honor system to which all the students have subscribed?

JONATHAN: Let's say it does.

PAUL: Then I would say that you have pledged yourself to report him. If, on the other hand, you have not made such a pledge, then it seems to me you are claiming for yourself an authority you do not have. You are acting as though you were not a fellow student. You are representing the authorities. In this case, I do not think you should turn him in. But if you have pledged that you would abide by an honor system, then you must do it; I do not see how you could then avoid reporting an act of cheating without violating your explicit pledge of honor.

JONATHAN: Shall we focus on the pledge for a second? I don't think the fact of the pledge will get us very far toward solving this problem. Suppose your parents enrolled you in that school, insisted that you go to that school, and the conditions were that you take a physical exam, that you wear a tie and jacket, and that you sign that pledge. That pledge was pushed upon you. Let us note in passing that the law recognizes that you were too young to assent to a contract. Why then are you morally obligated to abide by the pledge when you were in no position to accept the pledge and you didn't freely choose the pledge? I would say that a student forced to sign a pledge need not believe he accepted it.

PAUL: The student who goes to school because his parents have sent him nevertheless consents to live up to the conditions of the school. If the school requires that every child take spelling lessons, he must take spelling lessons.

JONATHAN: Suppose the school requires that for the ethos of the school they have a hazing system. Suppose the sophomores are expected to hit the freshmen, to make them walk down a line and then whack them with a paddle. That's one of the conditions. Are you in favor of that?

PAUL: I would say the student now has the alternative of either leaving the school or continuing there. If he continues there because he is powerless to resist his parents, I don't see that he has power enough to resist the hazing system. I think he either goes with the school or goes out of it. And I can see many different reasons why a student might not continue in the school. But, once he does continue, he has to accept the organization.

JONATHAN: Oh, no, no, I disagree!

PAUL: No child is in a position to judge a school's ability to educate it.

JONATHAN: Your view seems overrigid, and even more legalistic than the law itself. Consider an example involving a simple question of values: suppose the boy or girl had been in school for three and a half years and has applied to college? To get into that college he or she has to graduate from the high school. One week before graduation the school imposes something upon the students that is utterly repugnant to his idea or her idea of what the student or any human being should do. Say, engaging in some public humiliation of other students—or not achieving graduation. If the child can find some way out, it must choose whether or not to violate a minor rule so as to gain a greater good in graduation from school.

PAUL: You mean that, to graduate, the child may do things against the principles of the school? Perhaps even against the principle of ethics?

JONATHAN: No, I'm just raising the question, suppose principles of ethics dictate that the student should do one thing, and the school demands something else of him. The available way out is to absent yourself—to hide in some way. If you resist it publicly, you won't graduate. If you don't resist, you do something immoral. Why shouldn't you in that case keep silent and escape both? Why assume that membership in a school gives the authorities absolute power over the course, present and future, of one's life?

PAUL: I think we have to distinguish two cases. There is the case in which something that is repugnant to the student is characteristic of the school. Now in this first case I don't see that the student has a right to decide against the school. In the second case we have a conflict of basic ethical principles. I gather in the second case we have a certain ethical principle, say telling the truth, and on the one hand perhaps the school's situation and organization is such that the student is now required not to tell the truth. Let's say that in order to preserve the solidarity of the school he has to keep to that rule of not telling the truth in a given instance. Now we have a conflict of ethical principles. We have a dilemma which no one can resolve except by taking one of two evil courses. Similarly, in connection with an ethical good, one may find it impossible to accept it and another good as well. This I would say is what makes for the tragedy of human existence. A man may have to choose between serving his country and helping his ill mother. Another, say in a civil uprising, has the problem of protecting his wife and children and protecting his business. A third, a physician perhaps, has the choice of helping one child and not helping another, who is perhaps a little better off. In all these cases we have difficulties where a man feels he cannot and yet must choose between two right actions. When he is faced with these situations, he must make a decision one way or another and be responsible for not having done that which actually, as a matter of practicality, he could not have done. This is another way of saying the man is a sinner, that man cannot avoid guilt, or that this is a tragic life.

JONATHAN: The student in your example is in such a dilemma that hiding, silence, is no answer. We ought to reserve one issue that we both agree on for later discussion, I think: we both assume there *is* something in this world that is good, something that is bad, that there *is* an objective good, and that man's actions can in fact make the world a better or a worse place. There are those who do not agree with us on that point, and we will have to handle that later and discuss then how we both arrive at our belief and what justification there is for it. In the meantime, assuming, as we do, that there is a good, I think I could solve the problems we have raised without talking about tragedy and dilemmas and being wrong for doing something I can't avoid. Your view seems to me willfully paradoxical. It makes everybody in one sense equally guilty, so that there is no point in any one of us doing anything. My position would be simply this. In any particular situation I would try to discover what is the most amount of good (remembering the relevance of the future) to be obtained in that situation. Who will benefit, how much will society benefit, how much will the individual benefit? This requires analysis. And this is why we go to school, this is why we discuss problems with other people, this is why we read books: to understand how in fact to locate the possible good we are to derive from the situation. Therefore, when we come across a problem, a conflict if you like, of authority, of promises, and of obligations, our job is to think, and then decide what to do.

But, to return to the student whose dilemma we have been exploring, let me say first that you made a distinction between what is repugnant to the student and what is immoral, but I assume here when somebody finds something is repugnant it is to some degree on moral grounds. If an action is repugnant, it may be because he conceives of it as immoral. You have no right to say his repugnancy is not a reaction to its immorality and dismiss him. Repugnancy and immorality may overlap. So, to come back to our problem, I would say we are confronted with an individual who conceives of himself as beginning to find a better life for himself, or for mankind, and yet knows that his diploma is one of those things he has to have in this world.

Now, what should he do? It seems clear to me that he ought to try to get his diploma to graduate, and yet not do what the school demands when this seems repulsive to him. If the issue is that of turning another student in for cheating, the factor of coercion, the possibility that he did not take the honor-code pledge of his own free will, strengthens my position, that the child need not go along with what it feels is absolutely wrong.

PAUL: Now you have raised a great number of points, and I don't know whether I can remember all of them. But one assumption you made strikes me as quite false. If the child is not yet able to judge properly, certainly we are not to interpret its repugnance as equal to a moral evaluation.

JONATHAN: But if it's not possible for him to judge properly, how is it possible to say that he is able to pledge himself to abide by an honor code—and to hold him to that vow?

PAUL: It's possible for someone to promise to carry out a certain course of action which has been set down by authority, and yet not be in a position to judge whether his own repugnance expresses a genuine moral insight. But, putting that aside, it seems to me the issue is not yet faced. I don't see how any of us really knows what particular course of action is going to produce the greatest amount of good for the greatest number. There are times when two courses of action, though mutually exclusive, seem to promise the same amount of good to the same number of people. Then the dilemma cannot be escaped. It does not seem to me that it's an absolute good for a child to graduate. Not everyone graduates. Not everyone who is a success in the world was graduated from school. And sometimes it may be better not to graduate if one then is able to retain one's dignity, as you yourself have indicated. So I do not see that it follows right away that if one is to live up to one's dignity, one must do everything possible in order to graduate.

JONATHAN: As I understand it, then, what you are saying is that quite often we are unavoidably stuck between two choices.

PAUL: Yes.

JONATHAN: And that following authority has a virtue which ought not to be denied, particularly if there is a pledge.

PAUL: Right.

JONATHAN: Now, my position, on the other hand, is that the job to be done is to implement the good as much as possible, to see how much good you get out of the situation and how much good you will be able to do in the future. Therefore, I say graduating is a good thing, unless it destroys your identity or the identity of another individual. It allows you to go on in the world and be a more effective force for the good. Let me ask you this: would you say that it is at all times wrong to cheat?

PAUL: No, I would not. I think sometimes it is right to cheat. I can well understand how someone might be in the clutches of a tyrant and have in his care the protection of a great many innocent people, making it desirable for him to cheat, to lie, to violate the ordinary code.

JONATHAN: But I want to deal with a simple school situation. Take the classic question. Supposed a son has a dying mother who wants him to graduate from school, and there's one course he's flunking, and if he flunks he won't graduate from school. He knows he's going into the final exam in this course with only fifty-eight points. He needs only two more. Near him is the "brains" of the class. If he looks over, he will pick up the points he needs. Should he cheat?

PAUL: I would say he should not.

JONATHAN: Why?

PAUL: Because he is in no position to evaluate the importance of his act for his mother. The fact that his mother is involved does not actually change the situation; he has an obligation not only to her but to all the other students and to the teachers as well. When he cheats, he gets a mark that is weighed against the marks of the other students, and therefore in some sense he is denying a good to every single one of them who has not cheated; his mark which is exactly the same as someone else's who has not cheated is in a sense a way of diminishing the value of that other student's work and mark. Other students also have family relations; parents dote on them; others want them to make out well; the fact that they have the same mark as he has, although he is a poorer student, in some sense diminishes them; they will then displease their parents and perhaps to the same degree. No child can stand there as an eternal judge, as a God, and say that the anguish caused to his parent is greater than the anguish caused to any other student's parent.

JONATHAN: But of course anybody who gets over sixty passes.

PAUL: But you don't know what these other students are doing and what kind of conditions they are meeting.

JONATHAN: We do agree, don't we, that if a lie would save a life from a tyrant, we should lie; is that right?

PAUL: Yes.

JONATHAN: Now if a lie would save us from a tyranny of life itself in some sense, we would also, I suppose, be free to lie. Now it's possible to work this closer and closer to the situation we've been considering, by supposing that the doctor says the most important medicine you can bring home to your mother would be a passing grade. If she hears that you failed, it may upset her so much she may have a stroke. If you pass, it will give her the will to live. Her life hangs in the balance. To insult him by saying he's playing God won't get you very far, because every judgment you make assumes you are God in one sense, because every judgment makes the claim that you perceive what everyone else should perceive in the same way you do. In saying "this is right," we expect others to respond in the same way. But where do you draw the line and in what terms?

PAUL: Well, the child has many alternatives. One, to study harder; two, to lie to the parent; three, to alter the report card rather than to cheat on the examination. Why is cheating the only alternative? After all, he might get caught and the situation would be much worse. Not only would he fail, but he would go home in disgrace.

JONATHAN: You're admitting, in other words, that some form of dishonesty would be acceptable?

PAUL: I said that before, in connection with the tyrant.

JONATHAN: So we're picking the most effective form of dishonesty.

PAUL: Not the most effective form.

JONATHAN: The safest?

PAUL: The most tolerable form in view of the dilemma presented to us in which either alternative would be bad.

JONATHAN: What makes it tolerable? Ability? That it would be easy?

PAUL: No. In the case you gave me, the doctor says that the mother will die, which we do not want her to do at the present time. The other alternative is that I cannot pass. Therefore I have the choice that either I will be honest and fail and my mother will die, or I will be dishonest and perhaps pass and my mother will live. I have these alternatives, neither one of which is altogether good or altogether bad. Therefore I say it is a tragic decision. Whatever you do, you will be doing wrong as well as right.

JONATHAN: Well, to label it tragedy may not get you far. And of course there is the now classic problem that Immanuel Kant raises when he asks: suppose somebody comes to your house intending to murder someone who is staying there. Should you tell him the truth if he asks where your guest is? Should you warn your guest? How responsible are you for what happens?

PAUL: Kant says that it is necessary to tell the truth regardless. If we were to lie and say that our guest had left the house, but unknown to us he in fact *was* hiding around the corner, and the murderer went around the corner and found him, we would be responsible for sending the murderer to the very place where his victim was.

JONATHAN: But this example, resting on a far-out possibility, is slightly absurd, and not philosophical. His argument itself says that lying is such an objectively wrong thing that nothing can justify it.

PAUL: Whatever is right to do is absolutely right, says Kant; what is wrong is absolutely wrong, regardless of its instrumental value. No circumstances will change it. The good is determined away from the nature of the world. It is something absolute, something universal and necessary for all mankind.

JONATHAN: Isn't there some sort of compulsion in that argument? If the good can change from place and time, if what I ought to do varies and depends upon what I want to do or upon the customs of particular societies, then how is there any universal good?

PAUL: Kant says that the good has an objectivity which is beyond my own desires and the particular decisions of society.

JONATHAN: How do I distingush the conditions from the good, how do I locate the good? This is, after all, the problem I suppose to which Plato addressed himself in his *Dialogues*, and as you know, those *Dialogues* very rarely reach a satisfactory solution. People confronted with a problem like this cannot sit around like the ancient Greeks and discuss it. They must reach a practical decision. If it is this hard, what do you do?

PAUL: If you are faced with two courses of action which seem to be more or less equally desirable or undesirable, there is nothing to do but to make a decision. Recognize the fact that there is something wrong in what one is doing and try eventually to make up for the wrong that one is now compelled to do in choosing this particular way rather than the other.

JONATHAN: I'm afraid that this merely poses the question again. To say that we must choose, and then recognize that we have failed to some degree, does not in fact tell me *how* we should choose. Are there at least abstract principles? I think I could furnish some. If you can't, I think you have no way of solving any of these problems.

PAUL: I thought the case I was discussing was one in which, no matter what principles we employ, the alternatives seem to be equally undesirable or desirable.

JONATHAN: Well, how do we choose in the other instances?

PAUL: In the first case, you cannot choose by any principles because by definition the alternative courses are equal, given the same principles. But now if you ask, are there any principles which can help us make a decision regarding a choice of alternatives when one alternative *is* better than the other, then I'd say there *are* such principles. One of these has already been indicated—the greatest good for the greatest number. Another is to judge what is absolutely right in terms of what is eternal and universal. A third is to ask what makes for harmonious relationship of men with men, or what makes it possible for men to grow together, to mature, to do the best possible for one another and themselves.

JONATHAN: I would just like to point out that the principle I suggest is not the utilitarian principle of the greatest good for the greatest number but that of maximizing the good which is *not* defined as the greatest good for the greatest number. This is another abstract question for us to reserve for later on, that is, how in fact do we discover what is good? Are there in fact conflicting equal absolute goods? Is there one absolute good in terms of which other goods are derivative, and so on? But let us turn back to the original question. If you are right in saying that a student has absolutely no right to cheat, doesn't he then have an obligation to other students to turn a cheater in?

PAUL: Doesn't that put the student above the whole class? Will he not be deciding that this cheater is injuring not only himself but everyone? Now what right has one particular student to decide this question?

JONATHAN: Well, that's just the point. If it is so clear that he should not cheat because of his obligation to the other students, doesn't it apply to the other cheaters he sees? How can he distinguish this other person from himself?

PAUL: Isn't there a difference between making a decision regarding one's own rights and obligations and making a decision regarding the rights and obligations of another person? I would think so. One has a right to demand of oneself conformity to standards that one has no right to demand of others.

JONATHAN: How do you have a right to demand this of yourself?

PAUL: Because you are in control of yourself. You are a self-determining, self-criticizing person. But in criticizing another, you take the position of being a judge. Every man has the right and the duty to judge himself. Has he the equal right and duty to judge others? No.

JONATHAN: If in fact it is so clear that the principle applies to him, would it not be anti-democratic to say that the principle doesn't apply to other people?

PAUL: In considering yourself, you presumably know all the circumstances. In judging another, you do not. I would say you have no right to judge another person in the very same way you judge yourself if you do not know all the circumstances that you might know in connection with yourself. And this rarely happens. We can almost never know another person's circumstances as well as we know our own.

JONATHAN: But to return again to the issue of how we can judge how to act with other people, let me ask: what circumstances would you say would justify cheating in the classroom? I thought earlier I gave you the one easiest to justify. But you say cheating was not justified there. Give me an example under what circumstances you would justify it.

PAUL: I would say it is very difficult to find a normal school situation in which any person is justified in cheating.

JONATHAN: Then why can't we turn the cheater in?

PAUL: Why should you turn the cheater in? You are not the authority in whose care the responsibility has been put to see that no cheating is done, unless you have pledged yourself to the reporting clause of an honor system. If you haven't, then you are one student among others and not a representative of authority. Therefore, you should not turn him in.

JONATHAN: Not even if authority backs morality?

PAUL: No: it is the role of authority in the classroom situation to define what is cheating and what is not, and what the punishment will be for cheating. No student should take the position of the teacher or the authority with respect to a fellow student unless he is originally pledged to do so.

JONATHAN: But I thought cheating was simply determined, and not by who said what constitutes cheating. I thought there is a principle at stake.

PAUL: I think I agree with you that there is a principle at stake. Cheating is cheating, but the question is whether one who does not cheat should turn the cheater in, and I say he should not do so. To be sure, the cheating is wrong. It is wrong on the part of the person you have observed, but having seen someone do what is wrong does not imply that it is right for you to report him.

JONATHAN: In other words, you are making a distinction between your right to condemn him and your right to turn him in?

PAUL: My right to condemn him privately and my right to punish him publicly, yes.

JONATHAN: But isn't it in fact the obligation of members of society to carry out private morality in the public world? How else can we have friendships, society, law?

PAUL: But a child lives in his own world. The world of students is distinct from the world of adults, and it's a mistake to suppose that the child should act in accordance with the rules, regulations, or ethical principles of the adult world.

JONATHAN: In other words, if I am sitting next to somebody in class and he has crib notes which will affect my grade, I should not turn him in. But I'm driving an automobile and the same student takes a look at a stop sign and goes rolling through: then I should call the cops and turn him in? Just because in that case I'm not a student, but an adult in the adult world. That seems to me absurd. The one situation is as crucial, perhaps even more so, than the other.

PAUL: I think that it looks less absurd if you make the issue a little sharper. A driver who goes through a red light when nothing of any consequence is affected, when perhaps there is no traffic about, is in one situation; but suppose the man had gone through a red light at a busy intersection and endangered the lives of others? Even if no one was injured, the question remains, shouldn't such a dangerous driver be reported in view of the danger to others?

JONATHAN: What is your answer?

PAUL: My answer would be that if you are part of an adult world you have to obey certain rules and requirements, and if you are part of a child's world you will have a different set of obligations. That does not mean that there are no rules which apply to both worlds, but there certainly are rules that apply to one and not to the other. It's wrong for a child to act toward other children as though he and the others were completely a part of the adult world and its adult values.

JONATHAN: Would you turn in a person for going through a stop light if you thought he endangered other lives?

PAUL: It is quite possible.

JONATHAN: On what grounds would you do it, and when?

PAUL: On the grounds that he was endangering the lives of other drivers and pedestrians.

JONATHAN: But if you were a student you would not turn in a student whose cheating is endangering your own and other students' chances of graduating and getting good jobs? An action which may have a permanent crippling effect?

PAUL: No, because an examination and its marks are to be evaluated in context by adult judges; what they will do with his various marks in the light of the student's activity during the course of the year, the teacher's understanding of his character and what school means to him, and so on, is a quite different question.

JONATHAN: Let me assure you, as a lawyer, that the meaning of going through a stop light will very much depend upon the character of the judges, how good the counsel one retains, what jurisdiction he is in, how well he knows the judges, how he ranks as a member in that community, how well dressed he is, perhaps even what sort of deal he can work out with the prosecutor. In fact, I would say there is much less uniformity of judgment against the man who goes through the stop light, depending upon his status, connections, and the ability to hire effective counsel, than there is on a true and false exam graded on IBM computers, as they often are in schools today. That sort of an analysis cuts precisely the opposite way.

PAUL: But I would say, not knowing very much about the law, that nevertheless the law-enforcement agencies are part of the adult world. Each citizen has an obligation with respect to other good citizens, and the fact that the law-enforcement agencies are biased in various ways is a matter for subsequent rectification; it is not a justification for denying one's obligation as a good citizen.

JONATHAN: What exactly is this distinction that you make between the adult's and the child's world? Is there some sort of a bridge that you leap over? Aren't children moral creatures —or more important, aren't students moral creatures? They hold jobs; some of them can vote; they drive cars; some of them drink. What is so special about the student world? We're all members of subgroups, aren't we?

PAUL: My answer to every one of those questions is yes. It does not mean that there aren't differential characteristics of particular groups. It seems to me just as wrong-headed to think that students should be governed in the very same way that adults should, as it is to think that children should be governed in the same way that adolescents are.

JONATHAN: I am not saying that. What I am asking is where do you find a difference and what requires you to act differently? Certainly when you affect the careers of fellow students you're doing something more serious than going through a stop sign in most situations. Where do you get this principle of adulthood versus childhood and how do you distinguish them? How do you change your perspective and at what speed, at what moment?

PAUL: To take one issue at a time—the evaluation of what good marks mean in school is not, I think, within the competence of the student.

JONATHAN: They know it means graduation, whereas you do not know, I assure you, you do not know, what in fact the effect of the laws are in a particular jurisdiction. When you turn somebody in for a traffic violation, you have no idea of the sanctions to be applied, what penalties are imposed, how hard the judges are. But we all know in a classroom that it's a question of graduation or no graduation.

PAUL: Well, I do not know this, for teachers do not necessarily accept the result of an examination as decisive for graduation.

JONATHAN: There are certainly many schools in which graduation is decided by one's grades on a comprehensive examination. And then there is certainly a risk, a clear risk of not graduating, whereas you don't know what the sanctions to be imposed upon a negligent driver are, certainly as a passer-by, you don't even know the law most of the time, and very rarely do you know the type of judges, the type of juries, and the type of lawyers that deal with these matters.

PAUL: I don't really think that makes a great difference in this situation. You don't know the type of teacher involved either; you don't know the school authorities' judgment, or the college's admission principles. Nobody really knows these. These decisions are made in private. I think this leaves the matter ambiguous. I would suggest that we forget about the differences and the possible judgments that could be made about a given act and concentrate upon the act itself as being good or bad, and whether there is a difference between an act as carried out by a child, an adolescent, a young man, and a mature man.

JONATHAN: Fine, well, answer that then.

PAUL: I would say that there are acts which may seem similar but have to be evaluated differently, depending upon who performs them.

JONATHAN: That's a somewhat abstract answer.

PAUL: I'll try to give you some concrete examples of what I mean. A child who is annoyed at the way a game is conducted and walks off with his bat and ball is a disagreeable child, but not I would say an immoral one. A man who has a partnership and doesn't like the way his partner walks, talks, or dresses has no right to take out his money and say that the partnership is ended; if he did this, he would be immoral and undoubtedly also be violating some sort of legal rule.

JONATHAN: On the other hand, of course, you realize the law sanctions the latter action, and probably the unwritten law governing children's relationships does not sanction the former. That is, it's very easy to dissolve a partnership, and it is done all the time, but children punish each other by expressing their dislikes.

PAUL: Yes, but when you legally dissolve a partnership certain conditions have to be met, whereas a child can act out of pure petulance.

JONATHAN: And suffer the stings of the other children's anger. I think you're confusing two things here. You're confusing students with children. Are your graduate students children? You see, on the one hand you're talking about groups; on the other hand you're talking about how we judge children differently from how we judge adults. Let us separate those.

PAUL: Good. I think that is very good. I do think we have to distinguish between students at different stages and I would suggest that we do it in terms of childhood, adolescence, youth, and maturity. Now, the graduate student presumably, though still a student, is claiming to function as a mature man, and the judgments we must impose upon him are quite different from the kind of judgment we would impose upon an undergraduate, and certainly from those judgments we would impose upon a high-school student, and certainly different again from the kind we impose on an elementary-school student.

JONATHAN: Should *he* turn in a cheater?

PAUL: A graduate student?

JONATHAN: Yes. If he knows, for example, that another classmate plagiarized?

PAUL: I would like to answer that question, but first let me ask another: should one report to the income-tax authorities someone who is not paying his full income tax?

JONATHAN: Well, let me tell you the law on this matter. The law is that if you claim somebody evaded the income tax and your charge proves correct, the internal-revenue service will pay you, I think, up to twenty-five percent of money they recover.

PAUL: I know that, but I am asking you is it proper, is it moral to turn him in? Not whether it is profitable.

JONATHAN: Well, if we were to accept what you said earlier, that we must accede to authority, we have something of an honor system, if you like, in this country. A democracy can only function when an informed citizenry follows a rule of law.

PAUL: Good.

JONATHAN: In that case your principles say "turn the guy in; get the twenty-five percent." But my principle says that it's nobody's business but his own since no other individual is directly involved. The courts have ruled that no citizen has a direct interest in the federal government's money. I would not turn him in. I don't think it's your right to judge another man's income-tax report and set the state against him. I don't know his problems, as you said earlier. But I do know all the terrible things that may happen in his life if I do report him.

PAUL: Now I don't know that my behavior would be different from yours. More likely than not, I would not do anything about it. But if I lived in terms of what ought to be, I think I would have to report him. And, to answer your question, if I were living the perfect moral life as a graduate student I would have to give some kind of evidence to the authorities that the graduate student who plagiarized was not a bona fide student, that he was not actually doing his own work, but was in fact deceiving others, and in the end of course himself.

JONATHAN: In other words, even recalling the traffic-light example, the only distinction for you is the maturity of the individual.

PAUL: Right, though I do think there are some common principles. The child knows when it is telling a lie; the child knows when it's stealing, and the rules of lying and stealing apply to it as well as to the adult, except that the penalties and the conditions have to be taken into account and applied in different degrees.

JONATHAN: If in fact it is a question of maturity (and I would agree to some extent that it is), let us move our inquiry from the classroom, where, clearly, there is an assumption of lack of maturity, which is why students are sent to school. In other words, we have two conditions, youth and studenthood.

Let us go to the related field of athletics. Let's deal with two questions. One, where the athlete cheats in an accepted way—for example, hits people coming down from the basket in basketball; and two, where the athlete does something which he probably ought not to do, but which is not forbidden by the rules. Say, his doctor once prescribed Dexedrine for him. He runs a lot faster when he takes it, so he takes Dexedrine and wins the big race. How would you analyze those two questions in terms of maturity, in terms of an eighteen-year-old, say, or a seventeen-year-old?

PAUL: I would distinguish between amateur and professional sports. So-called professional sport is a business in which we have to deal in terms of business ethics. Amateur sport is designed, presumably, in order to build character. There is a contradiction or at least a paradox in the view that a man should do whatever he can to win in amateur sports even though this involves a corruption of character. Winning offers a test of one's willingness or determination—in fact, a test of character. So I would

say that there is no warrant for anyone's taking stimu-
lants in order to gain a special advantage while engaged
in the enterprise of building character through competition against others and against the hard realities of time
and space.

JONATHAN: What about "accepted" forms of breaking the rules,
like slugging people under a basket in basketball or
grabbing face guards in football?

PAUL: I would say that these too are to be condemned, and that
the people we admire in the realm of amateur sports are
precisely those who thought that character building was
more important than winning. Two instances come to
mind. Lou Little, the football coach for many years at
Columbia University, was admired by students, faculty,
and fellow coaches because his primary concern was with
the men who were playing for him. The fact that he did
not win many games never affected their high admiration for him. A second case is Bill Bradley, who was
recently graduated from Princeton and is commonly
regarded as one of the most outstanding amateur basketball players of his time. He had the admiration of everyone, despite the fact, or perhaps even because of the
fact, that many a time he gave up the ball to his fellow
students rather than take advantage of the opportunity
to make another basket for himself—because he conceived of himself as a team player rather than as one who
was to make as many points as possible.

JONATHAN: It seems to me that this is naïve. Little achieved fame,
in part, because Columbia broke Army's winning streak
after World War II. His teams did not lose that much. He
had great teams at one time, still spoken of by sports writers, and that is mainly where he gained his reputation. In
fact, if you read the New York sports columnists, you'll
find they were down on him in his last few years because
he did not come up with great men, except for two great

quarterbacks who later, I think, became professionals. As far as Bradley goes, there was criticism *because* he passed the ball. Bradley's job with that team was to win games. He was severely criticized by a large number of sports writers for playing the game in a mechanical way. Princeton lost against Michigan because instead of relaxing and shooting from the back Bradley guarded a player and fouled out; the whole Princeton team was demoralized. Everybody got upset. In terms of practical experience I think you'll find a lot of sports fans would disagree with what you're saying. Certainly his fame was based on his skill, not on his unimaginative fouling out.

PAUL: I know many would disagree with me, but I think it is because they think of amateur sport as a sort of miniature professional sport. As I see it, it is a quite different enterprise. It is to be thought of as part of the general education of a young man, and under conditions that are different from those governing so-called professional sports.

JONATHAN: Are you saying that winning is irrelevant to building character?

PAUL: I think winning is merely a test and not the objective. It is not the objective of amateur sports to win.

JONATHAN: But life is a very competitive affair, and winning is a good habit to learn early in one's education.

PAUL: The function of college is not to prepare you for life. It is to prepare you to be a man, and then when you are a man you can face life, whatever the conditions. The idea of educating people for life is a way of depriving them of a full, rich existence while they are students, and not allowing them to live in accordance with their own capacities and opportunities.

JONATHAN: Let me push this a little further. I said life is competitive and winning is a good thing because what we try to learn—character, will, and all these abstract things—

is achieved by the use of all our energies bent to those goals. If we are right when we agree that we try to achieve good, the thing to do is to learn how to bend all of our resources to that end.

PAUL: Yes, I agree with that.

JONATHAN: Then in that case we would justify, I think, the basketball player slugging other basketball players when he needs a basket. Everybody else does it, and the rules don't condemn him. We might find some case for the person utilizing every means he can. Certainly amateur athletics progress by people inventing new devices. The forward pass, the flip turn in swimming, the pancake in wrestling are not forbidden by the rules, though in fact some of these innovations were condemned because of their effect upon the game, like the flying wedge in football.

PAUL: I think there is a great difference between innovations which modify the structure of the sport and various acts which are not covered by the rules but are clearly designed for the purpose of inhibiting or injuring or taking undue advantage of those with whom one is playing. I would repeat: the objective of amateur sport is not and should not be to win. It should be to create conditions in which one can test one's nature and see the limit of one's abilities.

JONATHAN: Are special tennis shoes, special sneakers an innovation or a device in high jump? The Russians came up, as you know, with a special sneaker which helped them jump much better. Someone also invented a fiberglass pole for pole vaulting which shattered all the records. Now, on one hand it seems like popping a Dexedrine in your mouth. On the other hand it seems like an innovation. How do you distinguish them?

PAUL: The use of the flexible pole and the tennis shoes was approved by the authorities that cover amateur sport.

JONATHAN: In some countries.

PAUL: Whereas in slugging we have something which is explicitly forbidden by the rules.

JONATHAN: It is dealt with, but the rules are honored in the breach rather than in performance.

PAUL: Then it *is* a violation of the rules, and I am opposed to it because the object again is to play in accordance with the rules, not in defiance of them.

JONATHAN: But this slides off the point. Even granting that the only rules and all the rules are written by authorities, what I am saying is that it may not be so easy to distinguish between innovation and cheating. An extreme example is when somebody does something to himself rather than to his opponent within the framework of the game. The forward pass was something that anybody could do in the game, but Dexedrine was something that somebody could do to himself. In some sports it's not so clear—such as the type of pole, the type of shoe, or the size of a baseball glove. Then how do you handle this? Let's say before the rules committee meets. How do you decide whether it's fair?

PAUL: I would say the object should be to see whether the new technique or equipment is a way of taking advantage of the situation so as to increase the natural powers and achievements of the individual rather than to take advantage of some overlooked circumstance. For example, in the old days I suppose one might have been permitted to hide a football under one's sweater. This would be taking advantage. It would not be an innovation. But any kind of act which would accelerate the game, which would give more flexibility to it, would be a way of introducing a legitimate innovation. I think there will be times when it *will* be difficult to decide in advance whether what one has suggested is an innovation or a mere device to evade. I grant you that this can occur at times. But once we have decided that the rules are such and such, the fact that these can be broken without anyone criticizing the breach does not seem to me to justify an amateur athlete's breaking them.

JONATHAN: You might say that these are in fact the rules only if everybody goes along with them. You can also say that slugging under the basket is part of the game and attests to your character, just as in wrestling it may be a test of your character to edge off the mat even though the rules prohibit it—but it is the only way you can possibly escape. Everybody does it. It's part of one's technique to see how close one can come to violating the rule and still get off.

PAUL: Yes, I've seen that. In fact, I think I can think of an even more acute case. I understand from college baseball players that almost every one of them goes to places like Canada, Mexico (and, once upon a time, to Cuba) during the summer and actually plays professional baseball, a practice which is prohibited by NCAA rules.

JONATHAN: Yes, that's true.

PAUL: We have here then, in college baseball, an accepted violation of explicit rules. Apparently everyone involved knows that the rules are violated. I would say in this connection that those who are in charge of the administration of the baseball code have been negligent. I put the blame not so much on the students who are subject to this great temptation as on the authorities, who should now be more explicit and stringent in their application of the rules.

JONATHAN: At this point I think we can discriminate between three issues running through our discussions. The first is the issue of the age and the wisdom and maturity of the individual involved in making a choice. The second is the standards of the system in which he is participating, and the third is how much any individual should submit to authority; what authority means to that individual.

To return to maturity. What difference in deciding

this question does it make what the age of the amateur athlete is?

PAUL: It does not make any difference what the age of an amateur is. I do not see that we can avoid demanding adherence to the amateur code no matter what the age of the participant. There is constant confusion in this regard largely because mature men engaged in amateur sports have to have some source of income. Since their sporting activities are presumably not providing them with any income, all types of devices are employed, most not altogether respectable in my opinion, to provide them with an income. It would be much more honest if one were to define very carefully what the limits are beyond which one cannot go without violating one's status as an amateur player, and then allow the players to live in such a way as to be able to have an economically satisfactory life.

JONATHAN: I agree with that. Now we have been talking about the standards and purposes of athletics to some degree. Athletics are in addition of course a spectacle, a ritual; they are part of national culture, they inspire people; they have aesthetic value, all these things. They serve other purposes beyond building character. We treat them that way. We cheer for the old boxer not because he's showing character, but because we care for him in a way. Now recently we saw something which indicated this. Someone—I'm not sure who—named the highest mountain in North America after our assassinated President, John Kennedy. Mountain climbing is in general an amateur art. You are not paid much for it. But to commemorate a man whose life and death meant a great deal in this country, his brother, a United States senator, became the first to climb to the top of the mountain. If I'm not mistaken, he was flown in a helicopter to twelve thousand feet. He was not very skillful at mountain climbing. They carried him over things. Some accounts even say that three or four times he risked the lives of the other climbers. He did not know crucial techniques, like rappelling. Yet in doing this he fulfilled the standards and idealism of the country. He stood up for the country. He made many people feel happy. *Life* magazine had an article praising him. People in Washington, where I was at the time, thought this was a most wonderful thing. If I understand you, you would disapprove of this.

PAUL: Yes, I disapprove of what Senator Kennedy did. It seemed to me a desirable thing, although not of great importance, for Senator Kennedy to be at the top of the mountain when it was being dedicated. He could have been flown to the top of the mountain. For him to act as though he were a mountain climber, which is a very difficult sport, and do it in such a way as to risk the lives of other people and then appear as the first man to arrive at the top, before the professional mountain climbers who had actually begun at the bottom and who had actually climbed as he did not, is to falsify the entire meaning of mountain climbing. There are two things involved here. Did we want Senator Kennedy to be at the top of the mountain to dedicate it? One could say yes, but he could have done this without climbing the mountain. Did we want him to climb the mountain? I know no one who ever thought that they wanted him to do so. Not even he wanted to do so. Therefore it was wrong for him to act as though he had climbed the mountain and had in fact arrived at the top before anybody else had.

JONATHAN: I agree with you about the two aspects of this mountain climb but are you objecting to the use of mountain climbing as a sport to serve other ends?

PAUL: In part I am doing that. In part I am objecting to the deception that Senator Kennedy was practicing in the sense of acting as though he were a mountain climber when in fact he was not. As you pointed out, he did not climb the entire mountain, and he was helped by others to function as though he were a mountain climber. Nevertheless, the great honor which is bestowed on a significant mountain climber was given to him merely because he was the brother of the man to whom the mountain was dedicated. It seems to me that the mountain climbers and Senator Kennedy both were confused as to what mountain climbing is and as to what Senator Kennedy's function was there.

JONATHAN: Let me put the question a little differently. Which should we applaud more—a swimmer who is fast or a swimmer who is beautiful? In the old days Yale had three great swimmers: Marshall, Maclean, and Moore. Moore was letter perfect; Maclean was very, very elegant; Marshall splashed like mad. But basically they interchanged the championships. If the function of a sport is in part to supply a spectacle, should we not approve most of Moore?

PAUL: I think this is a very good question. I think what it points up is the fact that we do not judge our sports in all the dimensions in which they should be judged. It would be desirable, it seems to me, to give prizes to swimmers for gracefulness as well as for speed. Gracefulness could count for a number of points; the fact that we do not do this merely shows how we have been overcome by the emphasis on winning or breaking a record.

JONATHAN: What philosophical position do you think dictates that a sport or any activity has inherent standards by which we must operate, which we must acknowledge? Is that the principle deriving somehow from our notion of what it is to have an organized society, how men must live together? If that is the principle, I think I would go along with you.

PAUL: No, I think the principle goes a little further than that. It's what the Greeks called *paideia,* the cultivation of man's virtues. The object of education is to make mature, civilized men, and sports is one of the devices by which this is achieved. Sports require one to live up to high ideals in significant crises.

JONATHAN: Doesn't this argue for Mr. Kennedy? Suppose we judge his mountain climbing in terms of service to the country?

PAUL: No, I don't think so. I was just talking about grace in swimming as a good, not because it pleased the spectator but because gracefulness in the sport is one of the good dimensions of the sport. My objection to Senator Kennedy and the mountain climbers was that there is such a sport as mountain climbing. There are "professional" mountain climbers. Mr. Kennedy acted as though he were a mountain climber in this significant sense—that is, as though he were a "professional."

JONATHAN: Well, I will go along with you, but only up to a point. I would say—see if you agree with this—that sports, or any activity, require certain standards. The reason we submit to these standards is that we want to improve ourselves, that these standards somehow embody what the world is about.

PAUL: Not the world, but what a man ought to be.

JONATHAN: I would say the standards embody what the world is about too, because to swim is to exhibit what water is. To wrestle is to show what muscles are. It allows us to explore the nature of the world.

PAUL: Yes, I suppose that's true too.

JONATHAN: Moving from the standards which arise from what people are and the activities they engage in, let us now look at the standards and rules which authority imposes. Here, as I understand it, our disagreement is greatest. Do you think a student should sign a loyalty oath saying he is not a Communist, if this is a condition for his entrance to a college, or for receiving a grant or perhaps working for the government for the summer? In my opinion, it is an imposition of something wrong—against morality, I would guess, in your and certainly in my view. Now, should the student sign a loyalty oath?

PAUL: I would say he should not.

JONATHAN: In other words, you would say that—

PAUL: I would like to qualify that. I would say that it is wrong to ask students to sign a loyalty oath. But when the entire country, in all its institutions, is agreed that he must do this, I see no alternative for him but to sign it under protest and to take every possible kind of legal action to see that this requirement is done away with.

JONATHAN: Wouldn't you prefer to go beyond this? Let's consider a university that imposes compulsory military training, or a university that says that as a prerequisite for admission the student must sign a loyalty oath. These requirements are in effect because the government has passed a law that if the school wants government support the following things have to happen and the college president signed the contract. Is it not our duty to resist this kind of imposition? Just as we might try to avoid pledging to turn other students in because of its wrongness, or not follow a coerced pledge.

PAUL: This is a real situation many students must face. Landgrant colleges are required to have military training; it was one of the conditions, I understand, for their getting a land grant. It was true when I was an undergraduate at City College. It is true at the University of Texas.

JONATHAN: You mean they are required to demand these things of their students by the Constitution or by the law?

PAUL: It is required by the law which gave these various colleges sums of money; the condition was that they have to have military training. A student who enrolls at such a school must live up to the demands of that school, and he cannot avoid taking military training if he would like to go to that school.

JONATHAN: But now look at what Yale did. President Griswold

properly and courageously refused to take federal funds involving the loyalty oath. If he had not, would you object to the students signing?

PAUL: Yes, I would, because Yale is a private institution, whereas these were public institutions supported by public funds. They accepted those public funds and now they must conform to the declared conditions. If Yale also accepted such funds, it would also have to live up to those conditions and the students would also, if they wanted to go to Yale, have to live up to those conditions. The point is that Yale was not entirely dependent upon such funds and therefore could reject them, but these other colleges, if I understand it correctly, were founded with the understanding that they were to be government-supported.

JONATHAN: This seems unfair to the poor, but let me pass that by to remind you of something close to home. When I was a senior at Yale, I applied to Vanderbilt for graduate study in philosophy. I received a scholarship from them which I did not later take. I went to you and asked you whether I should sign the loyalty-oath provisions. I said I was violently opposed to them in every single way. You told me, "Sign it. It's not your fight." Were you wrong then?

PAUL: No, I thought I was saying the same thing just now. Perhaps I haven't focused it well enough. I say that if you want to go to a given institution you have to conform to its requirements. If one of the requirements is that you have to sign the loyalty oath, then this is what you have to do to attend that school.

JONATHAN: At that time I said to you, "You know I'm willing not to go to Vanderbilt," and you said, "No, you should not choose not to go to Vanderbilt because of that. It's not in your control. You should sign the loyalty oath." You were not saying it's your choice to go there and submit to the conditions. You were saying something different.

PAUL: I see. Would I advise a student who thinks that the

loyalty oath is wrong to go to an institution where this loyalty oath is in effect? The answer is yes. If the student has, however, very strong convictions as to the iniquity of this loyalty oath, he might say, "I would rather not go to such an institution than sign it." This is of course the decision he must make. I thought in your particular case you had some objection to the loyalty oath, as almost everyone has. But I thought that your own desire to study at Vanderbilt outweighed that particular objection. Had you a stronger objection, the answer would be different. Actually, I don't think you even would have had to ask me about it. I think you would have decided immediately yourself that you did not want to sign such an oath.

JONATHAN: I don't understand why it is the quality of the objection that matters. I would say something entirely different. I would say that it is good to resist this loyalty oath; it is proper, in fact, to make a big scene about it, or a scandal, if your rejection might make the authorities reconsider it. If signing the loyalty oath would be a lie, would weaken your moral fiber, then I would say refuse. But your position, as I understand it, is different, isn't it?

PAUL: Let me explain. I was a student at City College, and we had compulsory ROTC. I joined other students in mass protests against ROTC, and in protests to the newspapers and the magazines. Nevertheless I took the courses, and the examinations, as we all did, and passed them, because ROTC was one of the requirements for being in that institution and for graduating from it. But I did everything I could do to see that such a program would not continue to be required of every student at the college.

JONATHAN: I don't think that example gets you far enough. There is a distinction between submitting to an onerous and odious requirement like having to swim a hundred yards before you can graduate and making somebody do what they believe to be immoral. Again I might refer to the cheating situation. A man may believe that it is immoral to cheat or not to turn in a cheater. What I want to know is, when an authority dictates something that a student holds to be not repugnant only but immoral, should he submit? Specifically, if he feels this way about a loyalty oath? My answer would be that if it destroys you to do it, or if you're going to start compromising your principles, or if you think you can do some good by refusing even at a great sacrifice to yourself—then you ought to refuse. If it is not a denial of identity, or if refusal is not an effective form of protest, then you ought to sign. That, I thought, was your answer in all this.

PAUL: Yes, I agree with that. That is my position.

JONATHAN: Then let's return to the problem of cheating. What about the student who firmly believes that it is immoral not to turn a cheater in? Would you just say he's wrong and let it go at that?

PAUL: No, I would try to discuss why he thinks it is immoral not to turn in the cheater. I would try to indicate that perhaps he is arrogating to himself the position of a judge, which is perhaps not his right.

JONATHAN: But what if he says what you pointed out to me earlier? What if he says, "Professor Weiss, you explained to me that I should not cheat because it affects the other people in the class. Now that I know that, I want to prevent all the other people in the class from being hurt."

PAUL: I'd say the objection I explained earlier still holds, no matter how upset the student is at having seen a cheater. We must distinguish between the student as one among many other students and the student as representing the authorities by whom all the students are judged. I do not think a student has a right, by himself, to take the position that he represents the authorities.

JONATHAN: To another, related topic: how different, would you say, are the obligations of an immature person to be honest, to obey the laws of the adult world? Let me put it more sharply. I think most people go through various stages in relation to law, while growing up. Some break laws for the sake of breaking laws, to learn the limits of tolerance, what society condemns, in order to understand themselves. I think this is not altogether a bad thing. I might even say I think it could be a good thing to break laws if it allows men to develop themselves. What do you think?

PAUL: I would say it depends upon how serious the lawbreaking is. Is it a misdemeanor or is it a felony? Is it something which risked the lives and health of others, or is it some minor infraction?

JONATHAN: To make the principle more concrete?

PAUL: Yes, it seems to me that no student has the right to experiment, for example, just in order to test the limits of the law, by shooting a gun in a crowded thoroughfare.

JONATHAN: Or like Leopold and Loeb . . .

PAUL: . . . To experiment with the law by taking a life.

JONATHAN: But what are the principles?

PAUL: Clearly, there is no principle which says that in order to find out one's limits one has a right to break laws. There simply is no such principle.

JONATHAN: Let me give you my principles in this matter. Suppose we were to say we do not approve of breaking the law, but all we condemn actually are acts of lawbreaking which would limit your own or other people's potential for future growth. In other words you cannot kill a person, ruin his life, or destroy his property. And no person can do things which will warp his own character or life, but outside of these things there are actions which you can justify as part of a restless, adventuring, rebellious, and above all youthful spirit. Can't we say they are not as condemnable as they would be if committed by an adult? Do you agree or disagree?

PAUL: I disagree. The rebellion you speak of is to be directed at the established laws, and, as you say, preferably against those laws whose violation would not involve great injury. But rebellion isn't a good in itself. What is good is the spirit of adventure, of creativity, of flexibility, of imagination. I think a young person should be encouraged to develop these qualities, but when he comes up against laws that have the backing of long tradition and the sanction of experience, I think he is rightly condemned if he breaks them.

JONATHAN: Condemned morally, or condemned by the guardians of the system, if they catch him?

PAUL: Obviously he is going to be condemned by the system, and usually we will find that he is condemnable morally. Not in every case, but in most of them. But the point is that it is no valid defense to say that because he is trying to find his limits, he opposes whatever has been established. I think he does have a right to say, "I am an individual, I have spontaneity, creativity, and imagination which should be encouraged." In this he is correct. One should not arbitrarily and antecedently inhibit him or keep him within the limits of what the more staid adults experienced.

JONATHAN: I understand what you are saying, but I am not persuaded unless you include "law" as one of the limits he might step over too. Let me cite a concrete example. Part of the adventure and excitement of my undergraduate days at Yale was the parties I went to. At all these parties people drank fairly heavily, and that had a lot to do with making them good parties. The vast majority were minors. These lively, uninhibited evenings, at which one met and talked very freely with a great many people, were very exciting for the interchange of ideas. This was one of the high points of my career at Yale. If you were dean, would you stamp it out? It's against the law.

PAUL: Even if there wasn't a great deal of intellectual stimulation at such a party, even if the students were merely drinking in a quiet way to arrive at some state of quiescence, it would still be something which one might not necessarily interfere with. It seems to me that there are many things that are condemnable in society, but it is not the function of everyone in authority to make an effort to extinguish every one of them. Some things are not worth the energy and the effort to get rid of.

JONATHAN: But would you condemn them?

PAUL: I would condemn them, but if I were dean I would not do anything about them unless I saw that they were about to result in injury to the students or in an explicit violation of the current custom. Those in authority should have some kind of tolerance with respect to malefactors within certain limits, as today we have on the highways. Most traffic policemen allow people to go a few miles above the speed limit. And this seems to me a perfectly reasonable way of administering the law. In other words, I object to a complete violation of the laws and to a completely rigid adherence to them as well. What I would like to see is some kind of tolerance by authority and some degree of obedience by the individual.

JONATHAN: Let me point out that these may be very anti-democratic sentiments. When we give police officers the right to decide whom they will arrest, we find they arrest the poorer people. When we allow the individual police officer to decide what is disorderly conduct, we find that the Negro in a slum who mutters when the policeman walks by is arrested. But a rich white man who gets drunk and insults the police officer is driven home. Such discretion often results in anti-democratic tendencies. It seems to me inherently anti-democratic that we say teenagers can drink if they are in college, but not if they are dropouts. There are further problems. But leave them aside for a moment. If you had had a more tractable son than I, would you have forbidden him to go to those parties and drink?

PAUL: No, I think there comes a time when a wise parent

recognizes that the child must, within limits, undertake his own kind of experimentation. If he asked me, I would say that I think he is violating the law and that he should not do it. But the decision must be his own.

JONATHAN: I'd like to extend our discussion of the individual's maturity and his relation to the law by asking what you think of the new student movements in this country, of students participating more and more in civil disobedience?

PAUL: I have been concerned for many years by the fact that European and South American students spend so much time and energy on political affairs. It seems to me that during the years of high school and college a student is free of the grand responsibilities and has an ideal opportunity to grow to maximum maturity. These few years allow him to explore a few of the diverse aspects of civilized life, and train himself to choose the kind of existence he will eventually have as a mature adult. Students who involve themselves in political affairs, it seems to me, cheat themselves of this opportunity. I do not, of course, object to students expressing their feelings of outrage and injustice, or their opinions on all kinds of political questions, but I do think there is a tendency now for students to involve themselves too much in political action.

JONATHAN: I agree with you, but you haven't answered the question. Let me say where I agree with you and then what I think the question is. First, politics is not the end of life.

PAUL: Right.

JONATHAN: And if in fact I knew of a student who wanted to stay in his room and write poetry rather than go to political rallies, I would say "hurrah." To criticize him for not attending a political rally is to miss the whole purpose of education and perhaps even to miss completely what it means to be a civilized human being.

PAUL: I agree with that.

JONATHAN: All right; so we both agree about that, but now let's consider the Negroes in Mississippi, who have been oppressed beyond belief. For a Negro, finding his identity in Mississippi means taking political action. We would not disapprove, you and I, of a Negro student in Mississippi engaging in political action for civil rights. Is that correct?

PAUL: Yes.

JONATHAN: This is the paradigm. This is not somebody from Westchester County who thinks it's a good thing to make little speeches about Cuba while he's in college. No, this is a question of identity. What then do we do when the young Negro student says, my form of political activity is civil disobedience? Is he different from an adult who disobeys the law? Should he disobey it? How do we look at this?

PAUL: Well, I thought you put the issue very well before. He has a job to do, which is to become educated. If he is going to spend his time in civil-disobedience activities, when will he be educated in this broadest sense?

JONATHAN: No, what I am trying to focus on is the act of disobedience although we should keep its relevance to the adventure and quest for identity which underlies the enterprise of formal education.

PAUL: Oh, you mean does a student have a right to . . .

JONATHAN: In other words, a young person, a student, how differently do you treat his civil disobedience—aside from the act of political activity, on which I think we're agreed —from an adult's? In one sense it's educational for him, but in another sense, as you were pointing out earlier, it is against the law and he ought to submit to authority because he is youthful. But sometimes civil disobedience is the most effective form of political protest and is, in fact, condoned by many people, including conservative scholars like your colleague Mr. Alexander Bickel and respectable, traditional thinkers back to Thoreau. Now, can a student act on the historical tradition which says disobey, when that's a form of political activity?

PAUL: A man who practices civil disobedience is deliberately going counter to the law and must expect that he will be treated as one who has violated the law.

JONATHAN: And do we treat students and young people differently?

PAUL: In this respect, not at all. I said there were many times when the child, the student, and the mature man are subject to the same principles. When the student engages in acts of civil disobedience, he is punishable just the way any adult is.

JONATHAN: Let's return to some cases in the South. As you know, many students in the South have been arrested for and convicted for civil disobedience. Some were then thrown out of school. Some lawyers argue that these students ought to be reinstated, that they have certain rights. How do you respond to such claims?

PAUL: I think now you are asking a very difficult question about a problem which almost every educational institution has to face. What should be the attitude of a college or a university toward students who violate the laws of the community, the state, or the United States?

JONATHAN: And, in particular, students who violate laws which some of us might think are immoral and possibly unconstitutional.

PAUL: You're making it too easy; I would say let's make it harder first. If a student violates the laws of the state, whether that law be a good law or a bad one, does the educational institution of which he is a part have a right to dismiss him?

I would say, first, no institution has a right to dismiss a student until he is convicted of an actual crime. If he's been convicted of an actual crime, the institution is faced with the obligation it has to the rest of its student body. I think wisdom would dictate that in the political and moral domains, where the issues are far from clear and where honest men have come to opposite conclusions, the institution should not take any such action. It should take action only in connection with violations of the basic morality of the entire community—that is, crimes such as murder, robbery, and so on.

JONATHAN: It is important to realize that there is a whole new doctrine of law which comes under the due-process requirements of the fourteenth, fifteenth, and fifth amendments which says that a school board may not act arbitrarily or capriciously to deprive a student of his right to graduate.

PAUL: I agree with that.

JONATHAN: It has been interpreted to mean that retaliatory expulsions for civil-rights demonstrations, even with convictions, may not be permitted.

PAUL: Good, I approve of that.

JONATHAN: Now my point of view is a little different from yours or perhaps at first glance divergent. I think conviction for a crime is but evidence of a certain type of character or attitude. What the school ought to do is say what types of characters and attitudes it wants and then treat the conviction as evidence for the absence or presence of these character traits. In other words, the conviction itself does not get you very far, no more than a particular act does. The criterion of conviction is misleading and impractical anyway. It may be appealed and reversed. The trial might be postponed until after graduation. The reversal or acquittal might be on a technicality. A conviction varies a great deal in the meaning it has with respect to guilt. If a student stands up and says something terrible in class, I don't think he ought to be thrown out. If a student is convicted of some crime, perhaps even a serious one, he should not be thrown out unconditionally. All we ought to do is to take this as evidence relevant to whatever purpose the school serves. We ought not to say the school has the same perspectives, the same outlook, the same intentions, as the state in general. The school should look, independently, at what a student does and decide whether he should be allowed to remain.

PAUL: We cannot escape the fact that our educational institutions, public or private, are sustained by the society at large. They all enjoy tax-free privileges. The educational institution cannot hold itself in complete independence from political requirements. Therefore, it must acknowledge that there are certain kinds of convictions which not only turn the convicted into a criminal but disqualify him from being a student in the sense he was before. This does not mean that the student should be cut off entirely, expatriated completely, but merely that he cannot be allowed to be a student in the same sense as he was before. However, put this way, I think this is largely academic, for if somebody has been convicted of a crime, he undoubtedly cannot attend classes.

JONATHAN: Why do you say that?

PAUL: He would be in jail, I suppose, if he was convicted, wouldn't he?

JONATHAN: Oh, no, no. Not necessarily, not at all. There are suspended sentences; there is parole; there is release to the authorities; release on bond pending appeal.

PAUL: All right. I was thinking of cases in which a student was sentenced to jail. In cases like those you're talking about, I would say character is not the decisive factor, because men of good character commit bad crimes; it is the degree of seriousness of the crime which must concern the school authorities. If the crime is of the order of what may be called roughly "political-moral," on which good men might have divergent judgments, then I think the institution should not condemn the student. If, on the other hand, you are speaking of crimes against the social body, against mankind, then I think it certainly should.

JONATHAN: Let me give you one difficult question before I pursue this matter in a different way. Certainly one of the things

43

men have disagreed about through time is homosexuality. The Greeks did not condemn it, but in fact, if we are to believe some scholars, they thought it was a good way to educate the youth. Suppose we have two students in a high school convicted of homosexuality. Do we keep them in or throw them out?

PAUL: This is a very difficult question, something hard to decide, particularly today when our understanding of deviant sexual behavior has been undergoing a radical change. I think that I would like to generalize the question. How do we regard any kind of ostensible sexual activity on the part of the young? I would say that it is to be condemned.

JONATHAN: What do you mean by any ostensible sexual activity?

PAUL: I think any kind of sexual activity on the part of students which becomes a matter of public knowledge and is a public scandal is to be condemned. Whether it be sexual activity of a normal kind or a deviate kind I think makes no difference.

JONATHAN: You'd throw them out?

PAUL: I would say if they have been so indiscreet as to allow this to become public knowledge, I would throw them out.

JONATHAN: Isn't public knowledge a matter of chance quite often?

PAUL: Yes, it is.

JONATHAN: Throw them out on a chance?

PAUL: No, not purely on chance, but on the significant, though perhaps unfortunate chance that they have been discovered.

JONATHAN: For all sexual activity? Remembering that their youth makes it harder for them to reckon consequences?

PAUL: For all sexual activity which is allowed to become a scandal.

JONATHAN: I am familiar with neighborhoods in the slums of Washington in which, I would say, as a conservative estimate, over fifty percent of the young people over sixteen have participated in sexual activity legally considered a crime. They are not prosecuted because everybody knows this. What do you say to that?

PAUL: Fifty percent?

JONATHAN: Yes, in some areas. I have attended trials of juveniles in Washington at which a girl admitted the loss of her virginity at eleven years old.

PAUL: And is this situation an open scandal? Has it become public knowledge?

JONATHAN: No, not in the school community, because it is the accepted behavior of the individuals in the school. Everybody does it. Everybody goes to those parties. I mean they don't even know it's a scandal. They weren't brought up to think it scandalous. In these neighborhoods, when a six-year-old buys candy in the street, he finds the candy sold between rows of pornographic books. It pulls their noses right into the pornography. A six-year-old boy who sees naked women being beaten, women running around in rubber clothing, is hard to condemn for engaging in sexual activity when he is ten years older.

PAUL: What you are really pointing out is that there is a social crisis in the city of Washington, manifested in these seriously distorted patterns of growing up. It means that these people, who are being constantly exposed to and tempted by activities which are against the law and against society's judgment, need immediate help from educators and legislators willing to implement an imaginative and humane program. It does not mean, however, that this is respectable behavior. It means merely that at this time certain schools in Washington, according to your description of those in a particular neighborhood, must be understood to be schools of a different nature from the schools I have been talking about—the so-called normal schools in so-called normal populations, attended by young people from more or less normal families.

Let's go on now to discuss that basic unit in a person's moral education, the family, shall we?

2

The Family
and Its Members

This dialogue deals with the family and the individual responsibilities of the members. It begins with a discussion of the nature of the family and the meaning of family loyalty. The inquiry then moves on to consider the question of the respect and obedience owed, particularly by the children, and from there goes on to consider the question of punishment. It ends with a consideration of the way in which the members of the family interact and educate one another.

Paul Weiss takes the position that the members of a family must make sacrifices for one another, and that ideally they support and help one another. Jonathan Weiss maintains the family is a unit whose members are united by loyalties and expectations. They agree that a parent's role is to encourage freedom for the children and individual expression.

JONATHAN: Previously we discussed the problems of the individual in a society; what obligations he has toward authority; toward other members of the same community of which he is a member; and in particular what difference being young makes in terms of one's ability to evaluate and judge and act both in particular communities and in society as a whole. Now we might properly move on from that individual to the next obvious unit in society, the family, and discuss the role of the young person in the family and perhaps the nature of other people's roles in the family. Let's start with the easiest and most obvious question. What in your opinion constitutes a family? Is it defined by society, by natural biological grouping, by something intrinsic, or by all these in some combination?

PAUL: The family is in one sense a rather paradoxical unity. It is something recognized as important by the state. The law and our ethics recognize the importance of a family as a unit, as opposed to every other. But this very recognition of it as a very special unit puts it in opposition to the very state that officially maintains and protects it. The loyalties of the family are not the loyalties of the nation as a whole, so that every member of a family who is devoted to his family is caught in a kind of tension between his family and the greater world he must grow into. And, in the end, the young person moves away from his family to start a family of his own. So I would say the family is not a peculiarly or exclusively biological or sociological entity, but a distinct world with its own principles. We cannot understand what a person's duties or rights are in the family except by attending to it as something distinctive.

JONATHAN: That's not clear enough. When you say family, do you mean just the mother, the father, and the children?

PAUL: Yes, that's what I mean.

JONATHAN: You do not include grandparents, aunts and uncles, cousins?

PAUL: In the Western world, particularly in recent times, with the growth of urban population, a family is essentially father, mother, and children. In more leisurely times and in agricultural communities, it included a much larger number of relatives.

JONATHAN: You assumed loyalties to members of your family which are different from the loyalties you owe to other members of the community. What defines that loyalty? Do you think it is defined by consanguinity, how close you are in terms of flesh and blood, or by who happens to be living with you at that time?

PAUL: I don't think we can define a family purely in terms of consanguinity; we must do it in terms of the fact that it is a unit in which people grow up together and in its most ideal form are open to a certain kind of sympathetic criticism.

JONATHAN: Well, I think that's not precise enough. I think we have to have one of two things. Either one will do. Living together or consanguinity. If you have them both together, you have an obvious family. I think for example you owe a loyalty of some sort to a father or mother you have never seen, never been with. Somehow, because of flesh of your flesh, you owe a loyalty to them. On the other hand, I think that if you grow up with an adopted mother and father, you also owe them a loyalty of a sort. So it seems to me either one of these elements constitutes a family relationship. But you seem to be saying in some way I don't understand yet that they have to function together.

PAUL: That's right. I do not think family loyalties can be defined solely by the fact that the people involved are closely related by birth; for this can be a world in which each corrupts and injures the rest. I do not see how one is bound by any kind of loyalty to a family in which the dominant note is injury to everyone. Nor on the other hand do I think of a family as merely a group of people living together. That would make any asylum, any barracks a kind of family. I think you need both things together: some kind of what you call blood relationship and some kind of mutual aid in living together.

JONATHAN: Well, would you consider a Communist cooperative group with seven or eight kids, not necessarily born of any of the adults living in the cooperative, a family?

PAUL: No, I do not consider that a family.

JONATHAN: Why?

PAUL: Because you have left out the element of biological relationship. I think you would bring the issue into sharper focus if you asked about a child that's been adopted. I do think an adopted child becomes a part of a family. In that sense, we do not need the blood relationship. Therefore, the most essential element in a family is the process of growing up together in a kind of intimate bond which stands over against the rest of the world.

JONATHAN: That still leaves some difficult questions. Some people develop an intimate bond with some members of the family and not with others. And yet loyalty is owed, to some extent, to all. In other words, suppose you have a family with six children and one of them likes all but one of his siblings. He still owes, don't you agree, the same loyalty to that sixth child?

PAUL: Yes. I would say that the family first must be defined in terms of this mutual aid and interest by all of the basic members. Once we have the basic family established, we can certainly take care of our loyalties to aunts and uncles, cousins, our closest and more distant relatives, both loved and resented. I do think we owe a loyalty to them, but only because we have established the family in some other sense first.

JONATHAN: Well, I think we must go beyond this and talk not only about establishment of a bond but about a principle of generation as well. A true family that lives together and works together operates on the assumption of affection and loyalty for all members of the family regardless of one's particular emotion at the time.

PAUL: I agree with that.

JONATHAN: So it's not the establishment of a system within which you can operate. Rather, it's an assumption of the way these people work together.

PAUL: Well, no, because even when they're not working together they are growing up together. Although I don't think there was a time in the history of the world when there were no families, we can nevertheless see what makes the family desirable, and even necessary. The mother bringing up the child is not able to fend for herself. She needs someone to care for her and for the child until they are no longer defenseless. It might be imagined that her mate's affection is caught by the woman and her child in such a way that he stays on beyond the time when he is absolutely necessary. All people begin to love those they care for, those they help and protect. So that a man's affections are in some sense produced by his concern for the helpless mother and child. I would say, essentially, in its roots, this is where the family begins.

JONATHAN: And yet we know that one of the first major crises of a marriage is often the trouble that arises when a child comes. Each parent must adjust to a new lack of freedom; there's the problem of who should take care of the child. But I'd leave that aside for a moment, because I don't think the account you gave of the family's origins, whether you were speaking analytically or historically, really tells us enough about one's obligation within the family. I think you would agree with that.

PAUL: I do agree with that.

JONATHAN: So let's leave that aside. You implied earlier that you don't owe loyalty to those who injure you in the family group. I find that very interesting in the light of our dis-

cussion of the problem of when a young person may judge
what the other people are doing. I see a contradiction
here. The implication was, a person not yet an adult cannot judge entirely what is or is not of value to him. You
said that's why he has to submit to the school authorities.
Wouldn't it follow that it might be hard for a child to
judge, that it may be impossible for him to judge his role
within the family, or what is good for him or what injures
him within the family group?

PAUL: Yes, that certainly follows.

JONATHAN: Therefore, let's pose these questions. What would give
a child the right to stand up against his father or his
mother, or run away from home? What gives the child a
right to violate the code of the family and stand opposed
to it in some sort of public way? Say, for example, a child
refuses to campaign with his father when he runs for office; or a child refuses to look cute for the father's boss.

PAUL: Certainly, no child is really in a position to judge
whether full justice is being done to him in a family. Nevertheless, there are very ostensible cruelties which anyone
can judge. When the child is subjected, say, to actual
bodily injury of a severe kind, or when his entire future
is denied, perhaps by refusing him an education, or by
endangering his health, then there comes a point at
which the child has a right to leave the family. But usually, normally, the kind of training and discipline to
which a child is subjected is good for it.

JONATHAN: I'm afraid that this is not yet subtle enough, as once
again you rely too heavily on the belief in the obvious for
an answer. Actually, I'd go so far as to say that the whole
process of growing up, particularly for an adolescent, in
high school and again as he enters college, is a process
of rebellion.

PAUL: I agree, but only in part. There must be acceptance and
accommodation too.

JONATHAN: Take, for an example, the very familiar case of the col-

lege freshman who goes home for the first time at Thanks-
giving with new ideas and has terrible fights with his father. The father says: "Listen, son, I've been around a lot
longer than you have. You don't know what you're talking about yet. I once had stupid ideas like that. Now
don't you go to that political rally, and don't carry those
placards. Don't you start reading that radical poetry." The
father gives him orders. Now the college freshman has
these alternatives at that point: either he follows his own
spirit, his own muse; and I would say he ought to. Or he
he will obey his father. Actually, I think he should figure
out what his own muse really meant, adding concern and
respect for his father. This would seem, in your terms,
an almost impossible question because there are here two
conflicting goods of an equal value.

PAUL: I think in this case we have to look at the nature of a
college education. The father obviously misunderstands
the nature of education. In addition, he misunderstands
what his son is saying. His son is not actually advocating
these things. He is trying them out, since the object of a
college education is to try out all lines of investigation.
The father is wrong to prohibit his son's participating in
activities that are characteristic of the age and the educational system. Should the father insist, we must point out
that the father himself is contradicting his own declared
intentions since he wants his son to have an education but
is now denying his son that education. In this conflict
the son must make a decision. I would say he should
continue his education. At this point the demands of
family loyalty break down.

JONATHAN: I agree with you that much of a college education is
trying on new faces, thinking new ideas. In one sense, its
function is to say nothing is sacred; everything is open to
question.

PAUL: Yes.

JONATHAN: The experience has much to do too with learning from the people who are at the school with you, who come from different backgrounds and yet have similar ideas, or are from different backgrounds and have very different ideas. You try to find out which of those ideas you really believe in yourself. Even more than that, I think you experiment with a whole range of games you play in order to find out how many of these false faces really adhere when you lift the mask off.

PAUL: I agree with you on that, and I think it is very well said.

JONATHAN: Thank you, but I still do not think the answer we've arrived at so far is sufficient. First of all, let's go back to an earlier stage in a child's development: the conflicts that arise when the adolescent starts high school. If in fact what you're saying about education is true, that there are experimental educational experiences which the parent ought to recognize, I would agree with you. We can define it by observing what young people going through those experiences in fact do. In high school, a common argument that the adolescent uses is: "Everybody else is doing it, why can't I do it too?" And the father says, and I think sometimes with justification, "I don't care what other people are doing. This is what you should do. This is the way our family does it." Although the student may feel that what he wants to do is what education is all about and hold it against his father, nonetheless the father can claim the rights of family loyalty and leadership. You can't say that *just* because the issue is education the father should no longer act as the authority, as sole judge, particularly since conventional patterns or behavior are not necessarily truly educational. Moreover, we must continue to realize that rights aren't just items to assert and that growing is judging and acting on judgment about right and wrong paths of action which may mean opposing parents.

PAUL: There is a difference, I think, between the rights and privileges of a college student and those of the high-school student or elementary-school student. Isn't there?

JONATHAN: I agree.

PAUL: The college student should be the one who is critically examining all kinds of ideas, as you indicated before. The high-school student is not yet in a position to do this. He is still partly subject to discipline, training; he is still at an earlier stage of his development which will eventually bring him to the stage where he will be able to exercise a somewhat independent judgment. Therefore, I say the high-school student is not as free to oppose the parental decisions as the college student is and should be. The child in the lower school has even less freedom. There the parent recognizes the school to be a kind of part-time substitute for himself. At that stage the parent's decision is primary.

I would divide the child's relations to family authority into roughly three stages. At the beginning of his education, the parent's views should dominate. In the middle period, there is a kind of balance achieved between the parent, the school, and the child's contemporaries. In the college period, the parent should abdicate the kind of control he thinks he should have had, and perhaps did have, in favor of allowing the student the greatest amount of opportunity to examine the possibilities of growth in all directions.

JONATHAN: I think I would agree in general, but I think we have to pin this down further. I think there are some exceptions to be made. I am not sure that at any point at which the intellectual has developed any intellectual capacity at all, the parents have any right to dictate what he can read, what he can think. The forcing of religious ceremonies on the thirteen-, fourteen-, and fifteen-year-old seems to me wrong. I think it depends upon the intellectual development. On a precocious ten-year-old I would think it would be wrong.

PAUL: I think there are values in the family and in the community at large that the child is in no position to evaluate, and therefore it is necessary for the parent to require consideration of the things which a child might apparently dismiss, perhaps in good part because of some misinformation gathered from his contemporaries or from the public press. I do not see why the mere fact that somebody is intelligent is sufficient to determine the wisdom of his judgment in connection with such basic matters as religion or politics.

JONATHAN: I'm not happy with this, and it answers only one half of what I'm saying about intellectual life. In one sense, the way you learn is to be forced into things; there is something to be said for submitting to discipline or, if you want, going to church so that you are able to learn what your parents hold is true. But that's the conservative side. That is leading the child to knowledge. But what do you say to the father who burns all metaphysics and all philosophy, telling his inquiring son, who has just begun to read seriously, "That's mind rot, you won't believe in God if you read that."

PAUL: I think such a father misunderstands the nature of religious faith. He thinks that religious faith is best protected and promoted by denying the child an opportunity to think and to challenge. Faith is never destroyed by being honestly subjected to thoughtful and intelligent inquiry. The child who is not allowed to think about the questions that people who have no faith will constantly put to him will sooner or later find himself defenseless: he will be incapable of understanding exactly what he believes; and he will be ignorant of who he is. That father is not really helping the child achieve religious faith. He is merely blinding the child, and as a result the child can have, at best, nothing more than blind faith.

JONATHAN: I think you're wrong in terms of practical experience. I also want to make the question broader. Let me speak of the practical experience first and then broaden the question. When I was an undergraduate at Yale, I knew a number of people who arrived with strong faith and were subjected to questions like those you raise in your classes and to the questions asked by their contemporaries. Many of them lost their faith.

PAUL: I agree that this happens in college.

JONATHAN: There are even statistics to bear this out. Second, I think you have too much faith in man's reason. You can teach somebody very clever answers that will seem to answer any question satisfactorily. It is possible to instill a lifelong dogmatism. I think there is such a thing as a blind reasoning faith; that is, a faith that gives very good answers. The history of the world is replete with sophists and clever dialecticians who have never really examined the questions in the way others who were thinking alone have. I remember the old philosophical joke you told me when I was a child, that a philosopher is a blind man in a black night searching for a black cat that isn't there—and that the theologian finds it.

PAUL: I think we can distinguish between two meanings of faith. One is the meaning that I think you have now been emphasizing, the adherence to a particular church. But the sense of faith of which I was speaking is the faith in which one, with internal conviction and stable belief, actually acknowledges a supreme being who is the eternal judge of man's ultimate worth. It is such a faith that I thought could not be significantly challenged by any kind of argument. The first kind of faith is merely the acceptance of the general ritual, ceremony and creed of a given church. But, in any case, both this kind of faith and the faith which you had in mind are best encouraged not by denying a child every opportunity to think, to examine, and to learn. I think the parent who insists that the child read nothing, think about nothing that might possibly conflict with the practices of that faith has himself very little confidence in the faith itself, for he refuses to allow it to be subjected to any kind of challenge.

JONATHAN: Suppose a student hears about Karl Marx in school and decides he wants to read some of Marx's work. He goes home and tells his father, "I want to read Karl Marx." The father says, "I didn't raise my son to be a Communist. Don't ever let me catch you with a book by Karl Marx." Should the boy go off to the library and read Marx? I'd say yes.

PAUL: I'd say yes too. Again, I would say the parent who takes such an attitude does not understand what it is to grow up, to learn. Not everyone who reads Karl Marx becomes a Communist. Many of the strongest opponents to Karl Marx are people who have studied him with great care and found basic weaknesses in his ideas. The parent who objects to his son's reading Karl Marx makes a double supposition unconsciously. One, that Karl Marx is an irresistibly persuasive writer; and two, that the child is so feeble-minded that he is incapable of finding objections to Marx's view and so will be totally persuaded.

JONATHAN: But the young can be seduced by ideas, can't they?

PAUL: They can, but any seduction by ideas which is merely a seduction, a fascination, cannot withstand the critical scrutiny to which it will be subject as the child grows older and meets new companions and is faced with new questions.

JONATHAN: You know the Jesuits say, "Give me a child until he is six; you can have him after that." You wouldn't propose, for example, letting a child go through an intensive series of Communist indoctrinations at the age of six, would you?

PAUL: No, because then he would be unable to think freely in another direction. Just as I would oppose the parent who refuses to allow a child to have his faith examined, so too I would oppose the indoctrination of a child in some other position.

JONATHAN: Schools of religion indoctrinate.

PAUL: Well, they shouldn't.

JONATHAN: We do learn things by being indoctrinated, and that is the method most widely used. Do you think it's wrong for a father to send his child to catechism school?

PAUL: If the catechism is taught in a doctrinaire spirit, I think it's not really being taught. I think many a child has been disaffected with his religion precisely because of the childish way in which it was presented.

JONATHAN: Does the child have a right to refuse to go to the religious school because it may indoctrinate rather than educate?

PAUL: No, he is in no position to judge that. I don't see why a child should not be brought up in the religion of the parents.

JONATHAN: Then the child has not the right to sneak off and go to other sorts of indoctrinations?

PAUL: I think it's intelligent for a child to be confronted with and taught something about other faiths.

JONATHAN: We're not talking about faiths, we're talking about ideas.

PAUL: I think a child should be open to multiple ideas, but there are some ideas about which he is in no position to judge.

JONATHAN: I really don't understand your position. You are willing to let a child attend a school where he is going to be indoctrinated because his parents want him to be, even if he thinks it's a bad idea, but you wouldn't let him go off on his own hook, on his own impulse, to places his parents don't approve of, to learn things which interest him but may dismay his parents. How do you explain this?

PAUL: I don't want him to be indoctrinated, even in the area approved of by his parents.

JONATHAN: But you say he has no right to refuse.

PAUL: He has no right to refuse because the parent, presumably, is trying to broaden the scope of his imagination and of his spirit.

JONATHAN: Suppose he wants an antidote to the approved indoctrination. His father is sending him to Sunday school and he wants to hear the other side of the question. His father says, "You may not go." What then?

PAUL: Again, I think the father is mistaken. Now you ask me, when the father is mistaken, should the child obey? I tried to indicate this before: yes, if he's a child, he *must* obey; if he is an adolescent, he *should* obey; but if he's a college student, he *ought not* to obey.

JONATHAN: I thought we agreed earlier that he should go to the library and read books which interest him, even if his father forbids them. What's the difference between that and going to an indoctrinating session as an antidote?

PAUL: Because in the indoctrination one's character is being formed. In reading one is, presumably, being informed.

JONATHAN: Books can indoctrinate.

PAUL: I doubt it. I doubt that books have such an effect. I think books do raise questions and introduce ideas that one might not have taken seriously otherwise, whereas in an indoctrination the mind is closed and one is driven in a certain direction. For the child's own sake, the parent may prevent him from being exposed to an indoctrination. But I think it's a mistake for the parent to decide that the child should then be forced in one particular direction, rather than another, merely because it is one which the parent favors. I do think a child should be exposed to some kind of religious education, but the religious education should not be a purely doctrinaire, arbitrary one.

JONATHAN: This doesn't entirely answer the question. But let me make just one whimsical, ironic remark—if you believe in the truth, and if you believe people should have the truth, and if you believe that indoctrinating closes the mind to other paths, then perhaps you should not have written your books. Perhaps you should have indoctrinated me as a child.

PAUL: Do you believe you were indoctrinated?

JONATHAN: Not at all, but I meant to say that you ought to have indoctrinated me if you didn't want to leave me out there in error. Instead, you wrote books, which you think have no persuasive power.

PAUL: I do not think my books indoctrinate. But I do think they have some kind of persuasiveness. I didn't want my son or daughter to be indoctrinated by my books or by anybody else's books if at all possible. Therefore, all I tried to do was be something of a guide and model for you and her, which is what I believe a parent should do.

JONATHAN: Let me try to present a much more concrete case about indoctrination and the search for ideas. It is very hard to draw the line that separates them and perhaps one can't do it as easily as you have. Suppose a child wants to go to a movie. Suppose it's one of those 1930 movies with leftish leanings, or perhaps a movie which expounds an attitude toward sex like that in *Lady Chatterley's Lover*. The child wants to go, but the parent forbids him. Is a movie an indoctrination? Should he obey and stay home, or is attending a movie like reading in the library, in which case he may feel free to go?

PAUL: I think parents exaggerate the effect on the young of these so-called deleterious or deviant approaches to social problems. I would say that it would be wiser for the parent to allow the child to go; but should a parent decide that there would be serious consequences for the child, I cannot see that the child has sufficient judgment or wisdom to be able to say that the parent is wrong. The parent may be wrong, but the child cannot and should not judge this. I think it would be proper for a child to submit until it reaches the age of discretion and some kind of elementary wisdom.

JONATHAN: I wonder if your answer would be different if you were a moviemaker and not a book writer.

PAUL: I think that if I were a moviemaker my answer would be the same, because I can well see that many of the effects of a movie are transitory. I do not know of anybody who was radically changed by seeing one or half a dozen movies of a certain sort.

JONATHAN: Let's put the question in a different way. There are in this world many authoritarian fathers who, as their sons and daughters grow more and more wise, become more and more authoritarian. I find this very easy to understand psychologically. Such a father feels he is losing his grip; he feels his children are down on him; he feels he's losing his power; that they don't love him as much as they did when they were smaller and more obedient. In any event, he increases the exercise of his power. How do you think a son who is pushed around too much by his father, who is ordered about more and more childishly, or far more childishly than his contemporaries, should respond officially?

PAUL: I think you've already indicated the answer in part by pointing out why it is that the father acts as he does. If the son could be truly sympathetic to the problems of the parent, who is now apparently reaching a crisis in his own life during which he is less sure of himself than he has been in the past, then the child would be in a position to help himself and his parent. I would suggest that instead of making a complete break, the child should make some effort to help the parent understand him a little better. A good way to begin this is by trying to understand the father's situation, by opening a dialogue. Should it come to the point where there is nothing but opposition, and a war that goes on and on, then it seems to me the better part of wisdom and valor for the child to keep quiet in the presence of the parent and nevertheless find his own way of developing.

JONATHAN: Let me say this. First of all, I agree that there's always a war going on. There are four or five basic wars in this world. The haves against the have-nots. Some people think the blacks and the yellows against the whites, or between each other. Certainly I would say men against women, and children against parents. So we might as well face the fact that there is war. The strategy therefore becomes the question. I'm interested in the strategies. You say he ought to, discreetly, develop himself. Do you mean he ought to lie? A student at college may have his first significant aesthetic experiences and find that they are radically out of line with his parent's tastes. He may discover modern art, for example. His parent may be, like Khrushchev, a disparager of new forms. Well, should he lie and say nothing happened to him at school? Should he hide this part of his life from his parent? He has learned something beautiful, but if asked, should he say nothing because he knows that he may be held up to ridicule and perhaps even forbidden to pursue his discovery any further?

PAUL: The good parent's aim is the welfare of the child. Sometimes, by going his own way, in apparent opposition to the parent, the child will nevertheless be achieving what the parent ultimately wants for it. If a child finds that the parent is unsympathetic to and unintelligent about the basic experiences of childhood and adolescence, he must continue on in his own way. After all, he has his own soul, his own life, his own future; and it's just as precious as that of his parent.

JONATHAN: I take it you include your usual age differential in this; and refer to ideal parents and children (although it is not always clear when you describe the ideal or claim that it is really the case at root).

PAUL: Yes.

JONATHAN: But what I want to know is, should he lie to his family? Should he hide the truth?

PAUL: Yes, if he has to lie to be at all able to become a self-sufficient human being, to grow to maximum maturity— as his parents presumably had the opportunity to do— then he must lie; but only if the lie serves to free him from unreasonable restrictions that prevented him from growing in the way which is approved and recommended by those authorities responsible for the education and welfare of children of his age.

JONATHAN: Our discussion of a child's freedom to explore conflicting ideas brings us back to the difficult question of loyalty in the family. Suppose you're the son of a right-wing Republican politician, say a Goldwater or a Tower, and, the truth not being that hard to discern, you move considerably to the left of your father. Then you are asked, apparently on the basis of your ability since you've submitted an anonymous essay, to make a speech in which you would espouse ideas that could embarrass your father considerably. Should you?

PAUL: I would say yes, you should, and your father should not be embarrassed. Those who think it embarrassing for a young, growing person to try out an idea which is not in line with his parents' politics do not understand what that child is really doing. They certainly don't understand how a mind grows. Now, it's quite possible that people primarily interested in scandal and in publicity which would be injurious to the parent might use the son's action. I think the son should be aware of this and should see to it that his own development does not interfere with his parents' welfare.

JONATHAN: The facts of political life are, I think, a little worse than you assume they are. We Americans expect a family to campaign together; votes are lost when they do not. Let me make the problem a little more difficult. Suppose that the son, to experiment, wants to become a Communist. He knows that from then on security checks might bar his father from any important job because a member of his family is a Communist. Or the father might be working at a place which will fire him if his son is a known Communist. In any case, some disaster could strike the family because of the way society is constituted. Is the son free to go his way?

PAUL: The parent has made some sacrifices for the child. The child has obligations toward the parent. The child should be fully aware of what his decision to become a Communist, or to participate in some dissident radical activity, means to the parent and to the family. Now, if he has reached the age of discretion, and is able to make basic decisions with some knowledge, I cannot see what we can say to him except to point out again the injury he is imposing on the rest of his family. In the light of this argument and his knowledge, he must make his decision. Most young people will take into consideration the fact that they may be hurting others who have made sacrifices for them. But, in the end, I think we have no other answer but that one must make an honest choice.

JONATHAN: Let's turn the question around. Suppose it's advancement that's at stake. The father, in this case, is ambitious —in fact, overridden with ambition. He wants his daughter to date, perhaps even to marry, the son of some prominent family. What is the daughter's obligation to the father here?

PAUL: I would say one must ask some questions first: what is the intent of the parent? Presumably the wish of the parent here is to make it possible for the child to have a happy marriage. Now, if this is the aim, it is a good one. The parent's decision and choice of a husband for his daughter may be overlaid with prejudices and misconceptions. If the parent is entirely confusing his desire to have the child happily married with what are actually prejudices characteristic of the parent's own background, training, and knowledge, then the daughter must make her own decision, perhaps one in opposition to the parent.

JONATHAN: Does that apply to dating too? Suppose the father says, "If you date the boss's son, it will help me get ahead." Date him?

PAUL: I would say it is wrong for the parent to ask this possible sacrifice.

JONATHAN: Should the child obey?

PAUL: No. The father would be using the child as a means to something else. Dating can be a very serious emotional matter. To ask the child to involve itself in dating which is nothing more than a device to enable the parent to make more money is to misuse the child. The child should not do it.

JONATHAN: It may seem odd, but it seems to me harder to decide what's right when there's a less serious matter involved. Suppose the mother wants to get ahead in society, or she perhaps wants to serve her husband's ambitions. The daughter comes back from school or college wearing lanky hair, blue jeans, and looks, to her parents, like a beatnik. The mother says, "Listen here; we have guests coming over. You'll help me entertain. Everybody's been asking about you. Go put your hair up, put on that evening gown, put on those high heels, put on that make-up. I insist."

PAUL: The parent needn't speak so harshly, but I think what the parent is asking the child to do is perfectly proper. The family has social obligations. The child is a part of that family. The child has been brought up and supported in school by its family. Therefore, there are some things that the child should do. The child, I think, should not be asked to serve in this peculiar social situation all the time, but there can be occasions when it would be a perfectly reasonable request, and a reasonable child would accede to it willingly.

JONATHAN: Your answers may be too abstract. I would say an individual has a right to do what he wants—with some exceptions. One exception is when his action precludes the possibilities of other people's. Now, in the case we just discussed, whose possibility is more important? You don't learn that much from being a Communist; your father may gain more, may get further ahead. You must evaluate whose possibility is greater, which is a more important gain. Loyalty seems, to me, a major consideration here. Loyalty seems to me to mean taking the other person's ends as your own. Let me see if I can make that clearer. What I mean is, when you're a member of a family, when you're loyal to it, then you recognize that the goals of individual members of your family are to some degree your goals. Now, how do you decide when to act independently of your family's goals? I would say that one may generally do those things which are expansive, that is, experimental and educational. But those things which are destructive of one's dignity, and this would be a private matter, should generally be avoided. But the context within which you operate is that of your loyalty to your family, and in that context the other's possibilities of joy, progress, and dignity must be given almost equal weight with your own. I think that on minor matters of appearance you probably ought to give in, unless this is truly destructive of your dignity. However, on matters of thought, I think you ought to follow your own muse.

PAUL: I think now that you are more abstract than I. Taken purely as a set of general principles I agree completely with what you've just said, although I would think you could have cases where appearances might become a very important matter, and thought, on the other hand, a very trivial thing. There are many trivial ideas and judgments,

decisions of guilt or innocence regarding historic person-
ages when there are few facts, or a preference for one of
two candidates about whom one has little or no infor-
mation. So I don't think we can divide all cases merely in
terms of clothing and of thought.

JONATHAN: But triviality cuts both ways. If it is a trivial disagreement, all the more reason for the child to be free to express it.

PAUL: Indeed, it does cut both ways. If the parent insists upon
an issue which is trivial, on a matter which does not actually challenge the child's values, then I think the child
should agree.

JONATHAN: Would you say the son on the platform should say, "Yes,
like my Daddy, I dig Goldwater the most," when he
doesn't?

PAUL: No. I don't think a child should be made to lie merely
to advance the fortunes of the parent. I do think there's
no reason why the child should not be on the platform,
even though his political opinions are different. I don't
see why the child should not participate in a family
social event. I think also that the parents' standards of
dress and decorum are the standards for the child when
it is identified with the parents.

JONATHAN: Let's move now to a more difficult area. During a lull
in a serious family controversy, one parent whose reason
is not entirely clear may say, "Go ahead, do it. Don't tell
your father. You tell me." The other parent may say,
"Listen, I'll persuade her if you want me to. Just come to
me." To my mind there's something repulsive about set-
ting one parent off against the other. And yet it may serve
to advance a child's education and at the same time guarantee a minimum of conflict with the other parent.

PAUL: I agree that there is something repugnant when parents oppose one another in order to win the loyalty of a
child.

JONATHAN: What should the child do?

PAUL: Let's speak of what the parent should do first. If a parent is not out to win the sole loyalty of the child, but is acting for the child's greatest benefit, he should not begin by siding with the child against the other parent. First, the parent should work with the other parent, or work on the other parent, so that they might arrive at some kind of unified position. Suppose this is impossible. Suppose the parents are irreconcilably in opposition. What should the child do? Well, since they are in opposition, whatever the child does will be wrong. The only thing the child can do is to make a decision of its own and use the support of one parent in such a way that it does not increase the alienation of the other.

JONATHAN: Should you use one parent to persuade another?

PAUL: No.

JONATHAN: Should you lie to one parent and tell the truth to the other because you trust one and not the other?

PAUL: No.

JONATHAN: Should you try to influence the parent who is easier to persuade and create the opposition which may give you the freedom to do as you choose?

PAUL: Again, no; I don't think this is what ought to be done, though I think this is what one normally would do. I think the proper thing for the child, the ideal thing for the child, would be to try to persuade the recalcitrant parent. Not being able to persuade the recalcitrant parent, the child can only hope that the other parent would be able to do so.

JONATHAN: Should he request that help?

PAUL: I don't see that he necessarily has to have that help. But he could ask for it. Still, if he does, he's going to build up a faction in the family, the two of them against the other parent. And I think the parent on his side would be wrong to cooperate in this. Both the parent and the child would be wrong because in some sense they would exclude the parent who is in opposition from actual participation in the family situation. And the family situation is one in which all the individuals involved have to make adjustments to one another. It is wrong to have a faction within the family. It is the denial of the very idea of a family to have factions within it.

JONATHAN: My answer may be radically different from yours. Though in general I believe that you should utilize everything you can get your hands on to grow and to do the good, in this instance I think the spectacle of using parental disagreements for personal gain is so abhorrent and destructive of the family and love that I would not allow it in any form. I would even hesitate to use one parent to persuade the other. When the parents are so opposed that one is willing to fight the other for the child or to encourage it in opposition, then the fat is in the fire. The authority has disintegrated. There is no authority, no parental structure at all. Then I think you're free to do what you want. I think you should, in fact, do what you want and let the parents unite against you, if they will, because you're opposing both of them and because you haven't given in and used the sympathetic parent against the other. The fat's in the fire; the family's had it; do what you want.

PAUL: I don't think so. I think that the very divergence in views by the parents, who presumably have the same good interest of the child in mind, should make it evident to the child that the issue is not a simple one. The child should, ideally, try to see what truth there is on the side of the parent who is opposed to him.

JONATHAN: Sometimes the issue is simple. Of course, there are issues that are not, but sometimes, often, the issue is a very simple one.

PAUL: Let's stick to the simple issues then.

JONATHAN: All right. Let us say that a college student wants to room with a friend who is Jewish and left-wing politically. The boy himself is not Jewish. He is somewhat

liberal, perhaps even left-wing himself. The father forbids the boy to room with a left-wing Jew. The mother
says to the boy, "Well, just write me, tell me all about it.
I'm on your side, and I'll try to work on him and let you
get away with it." I think the father is clearly wrong, but
I think the mother is clearly wrong too to want to inter-
cede in that way. I think he ought to say, "The fat's in
the fire. I'm through with both of them."

PAUL: I would agree with the first part of your position. I
think the father is wrong; I think the mother is wrong.
But I think that the child himself should see what the
parent had in mind in trying to stop him from rooming
with that particular friend. However, we did say before
that a college student must make his own decisions.
Therefore, the issue, in order to be relevant, should
deal with a child still in a dependent stage.

JONATHAN: Well then, let's say he wants to go on a camping trip
with a Negro or a Jew. On the grounds of his prejudice
alone, the father says no. We may imagine that a group
of high-school seniors or juniors want to go on a camping
trip together. The best swimmer, or the best canoer, or
the boy who knows the woods best happens to be a Jew
or a Negro. The father says, "No niggers or kikes near
me." The mother agrees with the father. And yet she
simply says, "I'll help you. I'll hide the fact. I'll tell your
father that all the campers are white Anglo-Saxon Prot-
estants."

PAUL: Now we have a difficult case. I think both parents are
mistaken. Still, the child—now we have an adolescent or
just beyond this—is still subject to parental guidance, and
although the parents are mistaken, I do not see that the
child has a right to go out on this camping trip with the
people the parents object to. You say one parent is grossly
prejudiced. Undoubtedly this is so, but I would guess
that behind that prejudice is something the parent considers a reasonable opinion. He thinks perhaps that Jews

do not share in the traditional values of Western Christian civilization; perhaps he thinks of Negroes as not altogether willing or able to observe the hygienic or social practices which he as part of a favored majority endorses. He believes that there is some kind of reason behind his prejudiced attitude. There will be time enough later for the child to express his own independence and his opposition to the parent's prejudice. At present, he is in no position to do so.

JONATHAN: But what if one parent says yes and the other parent says no? He knows that if he is very sweet and kind to his mother she will try to persuade his father or hide the truth from him.

PAUL: A parent ought not to hide a difficult disagreement. It should be discussed.

JONATHAN: She won't.

PAUL: That's her problem. I think the son's problem is to present the case to *both* parents and hope that the sympathetic parent will be able to persuade the unsympathetic parent.

JONATHAN: Suppose the mother knows that if the father knows the leader of the camping trip is a Negro or a Jew, that's it. The boom is lowered if he hears it. The boy knows that he can talk to the mother and have her arrange it so that the father will never find out about it. How about going on the camping trip then? In my opinion, he ought to go on the camping trip. My only instruction, again, would be to dismiss them both, go on the camping trip, and let them do what they want.

PAUL: Now, I think there are really very few cases where parents are so blindly bigoted that no argument whatsoever will persuade them. But I can imagine such a case. We might consider a high officer in the Ku Klux Klan whose child wants to go out on a camping trip with a Negro and whose wife is somewhat sympathetic to the child's wishes. Now what should the child do? I say once again that if he's an adolescent or younger I cannot see that the child has a right to disobey the parent, even though the parent is, in my opinion, seriously mistaken in his judgment. Again, I would say that later on, at college age, the child ought to have the right and in fact *should exercise* the right of independent judgment despite the parent's firmly held prejudice and official position as a member of a prejudiced group.

JONATHAN: In other words, if one parent says no, that's enough.

PAUL: Yes. I would say a firm refusal by one parent far outweighs an affirmative by the other.

JONATHAN: Suppose it's an affirmative demand that the father makes, "I want you to go to church every Sunday," for example, and the seventeen-year-old senior or college freshman's mother says, "Listen, you let me handle it and you won't have to go." Then what? Does he go? Does he use the extra wedge?

PAUL: Now we have an ambiguity about affirmative and negative, don't we? I would put it this way: the decision that prevails is the one that requires the child to do something counter to what he wants to do.

JONATHAN: Why, that's crazy! That's absurd.

PAUL: Why is it absurd? It merely allows one to acknowledge parental authority.

JONATHAN: Well, in that case you have all sorts of new demands. Now you can ask *anything* of a child. You can deny him books, forbid him movies, silence his opinions—anything. Once you say go against what you want to do, that's everything. That's the whole ball game. You have no principle related to right and wrong.

PAUL: No, it's not; not at all. Before, we were talking about parents or a parent as a single, unified authority. Now we have a parental conflict. Now we are asking what a child should do in the case of parents in dispute. Does he side with the one who agrees with him?

JONATHAN: Yes. I'd say he does . . .

PAUL: Or does he take account of the fact that there remains a serious opposition to his desires? I would say he must take seriously this opposition to his wishes.

JONATHAN: As seriously as if both were opposed? Follow one opposed more than two together?

PAUL: There is something to be said for the parent who agreed with him, but I think the fact that serious opposition persists is something challenging to the essential stability and health of the family, and the child should keep in mind that he bears some responsibility for the preservation of his family.

JONATHAN: And certainly not participate by using one parent or blindly following the opposing one. There is a very difficult kind of problem concerning the limits of parental authority which I would like to raise now. The law says the child is a ward of the state. And yet, in daily life, the supreme authority in a child's life is his parent. I'm thinking of the sort of problems we might have when parents for religious reasons refuse to allow a blood transfusion to be given to a child when the transfusion means life or death for the child. Or when a parent doesn't want to send his child to school at all. There are medical and psychological problems which may not involve life or death but which are important still—like one actual case I heard about recently. The doctors at a hospital had the case of a twelve-year-old with a cleft lip. The parents had indoctrinated the child with the belief that God would heal it; yet the doctors believed that they should treat it now, for if they were forced to wait two or three years, the cleft lip would become impossible to correct. Or the whole great range of cases in which the state demands something, like saluting the flag, and the parent forbids it and demands something else. How do you decide when the state has the right to push the parents around and order them to do something for the child's benefit? When may the state order parents to do what it has decided is for the

child's benefit? And beyond this lies the question I'd like
to get to: when the majority of civilized people agree on
the correctness of an action, doesn't that give the child a
right to act in that way even if it means he will disobey
the parent? I might think so.

PAUL: I was coming to the conclusion that there is a body of
knowledge and of practical wisdom to which we must
adhere in the face of demands and claims that are based
on some special religion, or on special insight, or on
knowledge. When a parent refuses, against the accepted
wisdom and practice of a community, to allow a child
to have vitally needed medical help, perhaps even if the
medical help is only cosmetic . . .

JONATHAN: Let me make the case more difficult. The boy who had
been indoctrinated to believe he did not want the operation to correct the cleft lip was about thirteen, really not
wise enough to make up his own mind. Would you say,
let him wait three years, until he's old enough to decide?

PAUL: I don't think the community has a right to take the
child away from his parents and force the child to submit
to a cosmetic operation. This is a difficult, an unclear
area. Let's come back to it.

JONATHAN: How about a needed blood transfusion?

PAUL: I do think a blood transfusion is warranted on the
basis of the funded medical knowledge of our day, though
there are people who disagree, on the basis of their readings of the Bible and other religious works, readings
which, after all, are not absolutely infallible or unchal-
lenged by other equally devout people. Here I think a
religious judgment must be forced to give way, just as
the law made the Mormons give up their polygamy even
though it had the sanction of the Bible and the prophets.
Polygamy was thought to be contrary to the community's
—in this case, the nation's—morals. The same thing
holds true in connection with those religious sects which
deny people the use of essential medical services. Though

the child is a child in the family, it is a ward of the state, and the state has a responsibility for that child's health and growth and welfare. And when a parent acts against the child's welfare, as in cases of negligence and of abuse, the state steps in. I would say it should have the right to step in when any child's health is seriously endangered by a parent's refusal to allow the child to benefit from modern medical knowledge and techniques.

JONATHAN: Now let's get back to the question of a cosmetic operation.

PAUL: If the child cannot properly function without some kind of cosmetic treatment, say the correction of a radical harelip, or of broken bones, then I think the case should be understood to be like one in which a child is being denied its proper care and health.

JONATHAN: What do you mean by "properly function"? Would you order the operation for that thirteen-year-old boy with the harelip?

PAUL: I don't see that thirteen is an essential fact in this matter.

JONATHAN: The medical evidence in the actual case was that every month that passed made the operation that much harder and that much more disfiguring. After adolescence, as I understand it, the operation becomes more difficult.

PAUL: If an operation not carried out immediately would be impossible or extremely difficult and risky at some later time, then it would seem to me that the operation must be performed now.

JONATHAN: But remember, the need is only cosmetic, not a matter of health.

PAUL: I think we cannot separate the cosmetic operation entirely from one demanded for reasons of health. There are disfigurements which make a person incapable of functioning in public. There can be no doubt that, in a large sense, a child's health is endangered by a serious disfigurement which is allowed to cripple the child's normal development. Such cases of disfigurement, if they are of a sort which must be caught at a given age, should be dealt with like those which endanger health.

JONATHAN: Of what relevance are the boy's own desires?

PAUL: I think the boy's wishes in this case are not very relevant because he is not yet capable of evaluating what his lot is, and what will be the disfigurement if not corrected.

JONATHAN: I agree with that. What about acts which might be considered damaging to the child's self-image—the Mennonites' style of dress, the children of Jehovah's Witnesses who pass out literature, Orthodox Jewish children who have to wear skullcaps?

PAUL: I think we have already settled these questions, or at least dealt with them in a way I can't improve upon. As long as the child has not yet reached the age of reasonable discretion, lives at home, and is supported by the family, he must conform to the family's mores, values, sense of decorum, and religious outlook.

JONATHAN: But not in those matters concerning basic physical appearance, health, and fundamental ideas of education?

PAUL: There are matters in which discretion belongs to the commonweal that is in charge of health and possible growth. But the danger to the child must be *very* clearly demonstrated before the state can displace the parents.

JONATHAN: The child's psychological health certainly becomes a difficult area. What if we can show that the beliefs or duties imposed by the parents will cause severe psychological harm?

PAUL: If you can prove that, then I think the state has a right to step in and take the child away from the pernicious influence of the parents. And I repeat, if you can prove that.

JONATHAN: Of course these things never are that clear-cut, and that's why it's so difficult. I believe principles should be stated. I myself believe that the state can only invade the realm of the family when abuse and neglect are such as to cause physical harm. I would not let it intrude on psychological or moral matters since I trust neither psychiatrists nor judges in such areas—although education and pressure to create autonomy for the young is a good practice. But these issues are difficult and distinctions hard to draw.

PAUL: Yes. It is most difficult to draw the line beyond which a child is misused.

When you were a little child, we used to ask you to help mow the lawn, but instead of giving you some money, as many other parents did, we said that you had a sufficient allowance and that this was one of your familial obligations. Was that a good judgment on our part, or were we treating you so differently from every other child in the community that you felt embarrassed and thought you were being used unjustly?

JONATHAN: Well, I think first of all it wasn't uncommon, but even if it had been, I think it was the right decision for the reasons you indicated before, that is, that as a member of the family group one has certain rights and certain duties. In this instance, the rights seem to me to be the allowance; the duty is to help out. Also, there is something very wrong, I think, about a family bribing a child. Looking back, I think I would have felt a little humiliated by payment for work. Now there were special chores. I remember once I carried a whole cord of wood into the basement; hired workers would have charged three dollars for that, and I did it for a dollar. I liked the labor. The dollar was more of a token of respect, an indication that I had done a good workmanlike job, rather than actual payment, I think.

PAUL: I think that is a very good point. In other words, it is possible for a parent to give a child money for work he has done, but the parent should think of this as a kind of token of respect rather than as an outright payment or as a bribe that might be given to a stranger.

JONATHAN: Well, I believe we've dealt with what is an acceptable reward for a child's work. Now there's the question of punishment. When do you think a parent has the right to punish a child? What sorts of punishments do you think are appropriate for different ages and different offenses? What is the range?

PAUL: By punishment, you don't mean merely corporal punishment, do you, but also denial of privileges and things of that sort?

JONATHAN: The whole range. I mean, what do you do from the time a baby starts to misbehave?

PAUL: Familial education is in part a disciplining. Disciplining involves denials, what might roughly be called punishments, not necessarily corporal, but the taking away of privileges, such as permission to go to the movies, to stay out at night, to use the family car, and the like. This is part of the process of educating a person properly. When exactly is it eminently desirable to put some kind of restraint on a young person so that he will know what his proper limits are? No one can say this in advance. We can, however, indicate that it is a mistake on the part of parents to decide that no restraint will ever be imposed on the child. Every child needs guidance. It's also a mistake on the part of the parents to put such severe restraints upon the child as to provoke rebellion and resentment. The whole object of punishment in its broadest sense is to help the child to grow within the limitations experience seems to show are necessary for the greatest maturation and the richest possible adult life.

JONATHAN: My answer would be somewhat different. Let me say, though, that this is what I have learned from your example rather than your statements. From the age of about fourteen on, you more or less treated me as an adult. You never, ever, deprived me of anything, like the use of the car or the right to go to the movies. I can never remember ever being told, "If you disobey me, I will deprive you of this or that." I just do not have any memory of anything like that and I think that's the right way to operate. Let me say that a lot of what I'm saying sounds as if I'm opposed to you, but was in fact learned from you.

PAUL: But I did impose certain kinds of restraints.

JONATHAN: But we're talking about punishment. You never punished me with denials or anger, for example.

PAUL: I had already built in a kind of restraint which was part of the discipline; I refused to participate in your activities when I was tired or when I thought that I had already given too much of my time to you. Though it wasn't obtrusive, nevertheless certain kinds of restraint were being imposed.

JONATHAN: I think the reason for the restraint—and I accept it on those terms—was that you insisted upon your own identity, that you were not only a parent caring for me, but also an individual with your own rights.

PAUL: That's true.

JONATHAN: But I was in the process of outlining my own theories on discipline. First off, let me say that I think corporal punishment is always unjustified. Evidence offered by psychologists and psychiatrists suggests that it's a terribly risky thing. There's evidence also that what stops a young child is whatever the parents' absolute no is. A psychologist I know told me the following fact. Psychologists say that as parents they are themselves practically always too permissive; they let their kids do too much. But the one thing a psychologist's child never does is break into a conference room where his father is seeing a patient, not really because he thinks his father would *do* anything to him but because he knows that is where the parent has drawn an absolute line. Whenever the parent draws an absolute line and lets the child know what the absolute no is, there the child stops. The current belief is that corporal punishment causes emotional scars and is therefore a bad procedure, in addition to being a revolting spectacle.

PAUL: All I can say to that is that I myself was subject to corporal punishment as a child, and I never resented it, because I knew my father resorted to it at times when I richly deserved it. I believe I recognized that at the time. Perhaps I do exhibit various scars from that experience, but if I do, I do not recognize them. I would say too that it is a risky thing, but I do not see it is necessarily to be avoided in every case.

JONATHAN: The answer is that it is only one among many methods, and yet the most risky one—far more risky than the absolute no. Let me suggest that your non-recognition of scars may merely prove the greater wisdom of psychoanalysis as opposed to self-analysis.

PAUL: Oh, I don't know. That begs the question.

JONATHAN: I'm saying that the one thing we do not, cannot recognize in ourselves are our psychological scars and what caused them. That's why people go to psychoanalysts. The fact that you don't recognize the scars you retain as a result of corporal punishment does not advance your argument.

PAUL: Well, maybe I do have them, and just don't see them. I do agree it would be desirable to have absolute prohibitions made clear to the child. But sometimes a child will violate those absolute noes, and nothing but some kind of sharp admonition, perhaps in the form of corporal punishment, will be effective. I agree with you that for the most part it does not help, but I can well imagine that there might be cases where it is called for.

JONATHAN: I can imagine no such cases. I can't tell the difference between sharp admonitions and absolute noes. Do you have some examples?

PAUL: Yes. When a doctor's child persistently breaks into his father's consulting room and no amount of talk with the child seems to prevent him from doing it, it might be eminently desirable for the child to receive a sharp smack at the crucial moment which will bring it up short.

JONATHAN: Suppose the child persists? What then? Beat him until he's not able to walk?

PAUL: No, I would not say so. I don't think that corporal punishment is the only solution to a problem. All I say is that it may sometimes bring the child up short and be effective in a way other methods are not. I do not see that anybody knows enough about child discipline to be able to say in all cases that it is wrong to subject a child to any kind of corporal punishment.

JONATHAN: I think we can say so, and I think there is a body of evidence to support such a stand.

PAUL: Where?

JONATHAN: Psychiatrists. Anna Freud's work in particular. The general theory that I'm working from might be explained as follows. As a person grows up, he begins to recognize other persons' rights more and more. This is the basis on which you in fact give out rewards and punishments. Rather than insisting upon authority, each individual—the parent included—insists upon his rights.

PAUL: I agree.

JONATHAN: You let the child know that you disapprove of those things that inconvenience you. You insist upon your own rights. You insist upon them more and more as the child grows in understanding. When he bothers you, you act disturbed. You say, "Please don't do that; it disturbs me." Then, if necessary, you enforce it. You lock the conference-room door. I don't think you ever need impose powerful sanctions or the entire authority or muscle that you have. You can restrain the child, prevent it, because you have a right to insist upon your own rights. For the rest, I believe in freedom.

PAUL: I think for the most part I agree with you, except I do think you make an arbitrary prohibition against the use of one device in disciplining people. Although I think what you say is largely correct, it seems to me just wrong to antecedently rule out one particular method.

JONATHAN: I was speaking more broadly and saying in general I'm opposed to refusals, to deprivations; and in particular I absolutely refuse to condone corporal punishment. Corporal punishment tends to mushroom. That's one of its worst characteristics. A slap turns into a beating.

PAUL: Not necessarily.

JONATHAN: That is the experience of mankind.

PAUL: I don't think so.

JONATHAN: Well, psychiatrists disagree with you. And I must say I do too, most emphatically.

PAUL: That's your privilege.

JONATHAN: Let's move on to a couple of other questions involving obligations. Let us suppose there is a family in which the oldest son or the oldest daughter, through great sacrifice, is put through college. What is his or her obligation to the parents in their old age, or to the rest of the family, to putting the rest of the little kiddies through school?

PAUL: I would say that the fact that the child has been put through college, even if it was done at considerable sacrifice on the part of the parents, does not create a special obligation toward them or to the other children. That obligation was there whether the child was put through college or not. The obligation is a familial obligation, not an obligation which comes into being because of a particular thing that is done for the child. Your obligation is not predicated upon the particular opportunity that was provided for you. It's predicated solely on the fact that you are a member of that family, and if this is overlooked—and it is overlooked very often by parents— the child goes to college burdened with obligations which are usually too much for him to cope with at that point in his life. A child's life can be crippled and distorted because of this mistaken idea that he has a special obligation with respect to the parents and the other children. The child has no special obligation, only the same obligation that all children have. If the child, because of his advantages, should later become able to help in a way the others are not, he should of course help the family in a way proportionate to his advantages.

JONATHAN: I think what you're saying in general is right, but the question can be made more difficult. Suppose the parents say to the oldest boy or girl, "Look, we have a limited amount of resources. We want to send all the children through college. We love each and every one of you equally. Now our proposal is that instead of giving everybody a few hundred dollars and asking them to work through college, we'll give you all the money we have now, so you won't have to work while you're in college. When you get out of school, you should then take a couple of years off and work to put the other kids through." This would be a contract of sorts, in your terms, a pledge.

PAUL: Right, this could be a kind of family agreement, a plan the family agrees upon in advance. I don't think though that such an agreement is the wisest way to deal with the problem. By telling the child in advance that he has this obligation, you give that child a heavy burden to carry while he is going through school. But should this agreement exist, then the child is obligated to carry it out.

JONATHAN: Suppose he doesn't know there was an agreement. Suppose later on the parents say, "Well, you should have realized . . . " He goes blithely through school, and then the parents say, "Look, we don't have any money to send your brothers to school." Or suppose the family is stricken by some financial disaster and they say, "If we had had no money before you went to college, we would have made this agreement with you." What are the individual's obligations in that case? Would that change your estimate of his obligations?

PAUL: No, because I would refer again to his natural, uncontracted obligation to the family as a whole.

JONATHAN: But this answer doesn't face the facts in the situation.

The facts are that the son or daughter has graduated from college and then his parents say, "Well, there was an implicit agreement. There would have been an explicit one if we had been poor before you entered." Or they might say, "You should have realized there was an agreement."

PAUL: I would say that the child, now a young adult who has graduated from college, should be aware that he is a member of a family; but the primary consideration here is not that he was put through college but that he has an advantage, and this advantage enables him to be of greater assistance to the family than its other members can be.

JONATHAN: In other words, the existence of an agreement has to be clear ahead of time.

PAUL: No.

JONATHAN: You seem to suggest that if he didn't know about the agreement you wouldn't hold him to obey it.

PAUL: No, I'm saying that even if he didn't know it, he still has a responsibility.

JONATHAN: I thought we agreed that if there was an agreement the child must act differently than he would if there were no agreement.

PAUL: That's right.

JONATHAN: Good. Now, I'm saying suppose he doesn't know about that agreement?

PAUL: I would say if the child does not know about the agreement, then in some basic sense he has been very badly brought up. He should have known that he was being given special privileges.

JONATHAN: Then, if not having seen the agreement is his fault, he ought to obey it; and if it is their fault, for raising him badly, he ought not to obey it?

PAUL: No, if he is raised badly, he probably contributed to it. Don't forget that in a family everybody contributes to the final outcome. The child educates the parents; the parents educate the child; the children educate one another. This

is the way a family grows, and therefore if a child is badly
brought up, you cannot attribute it solely to the parents.
In our time particularly, there is a tendency to blame
only the parents for the failures of their children. This
is not altogether just. The parents have responsibilities,
to be sure. The parents are guilty, but they are not the
only ones who are guilty. A family is constituted of all
its members. All contribute. If there is failure, the failure
is to be accredited to all the members of the family, including the unfortunate victim.

JONATHAN: I think you may agree that the success of a child's upbringing is somehow beyond anyone's complete control.
It is a matter of breaks. That is, you can treat a child
badly and yet the kid survives, perhaps because you hit
him, for example, luckily, at the harmless times in his
development. Or, conversely, you can be very, very good
as a member of the family, and yet the child can be ruined
because you struck or punished him at the wrong time.

PAUL: That is quite right. No one really knows exactly what
the effect of any action will be upon a growing child. In
the best of circumstances, a child may hear an idle remark, a statement of no great significance, but he may
hear it at a crucial time, so that the remark has a very
serious effect. And another child, brought up in a house-
hold where the language used is rough and the customs
are crude, may nevertheless acquire an unusual sensitiv-
ity, largely because of the acuteness of his observation and
the fact that somehow, in this rough and ready environ-
ment, he has a freedom and an independence he otherwise would not have.

JONATHAN: I would like to add two things to that. The first is that
every individual must accept his responsibility for the
choices he made which shaped his personality. You educate yourself. You're alone in your privacy; you pick
your classmates at school and you listen to your teachers
in various ways. The second thing I would add is that

because parents have had more experiences, because they know what's going to happen, your job as a parent is to increase the maximum number of possibilities for the child's having good experiences and decrease the number of experiences which might cause him psychological harm. That seems to me the appropriate way to deal with any child. Do we agree on this?

PAUL: Yes, I think we do. Turning back to the family, though, I think we can sum up with the observation that everyone in the family, parents and children, in different ways and degrees, share a responsibility for everyone in the family.

3

Politics and the State

This dialogue centers on the nature of society and the state, and the role and obligations of the individual in both. State, nation, and cultures are dealt with in terms of the possibility and method of distinguishing and exploring their natures. The state of tyranny and slavery and the role of the citizen are then examined. The discussion moves on to consider the compatability and value of capitalism, democracy, pluralism, and communism. The role of the artist in politics, and his basic tasks, is also considered. The final question concerns the meaning and value of the state and the citizen's duties with respect to it in terms of that value and meaning.

Paul Weiss makes a rather sharp distinction between the nature and tasks of a state and the people. He puts considerable emphasis on the place of tradition. Jonathan Weiss defends an implicit social-contract theory. In his view, the citizens rely on common institutions and a faith in a common value and response to define the tasks of the state and the rights of the citizens. They agree that it is the function of the state to do for men what they cannot do for themselves individually.

JONATHAN: In the previous chapters we discussed the individual, particularly the young individual and what obligations he may have in regard to other individuals. In the second chapter we discussed the family, the obligations involved there, the meaning the family has. Now we ought to move to a bigger area and a broader spectrum; that is, the community of individuals living together in what is called the state. In the following chapter we will be moving to what we call, more broadly perhaps, society and culture in general. In this particular chapter we will deal with the state as an entity. In your opinion what defines a state?

PAUL: A state is to be distinguished from a society in that it is governed by positive law; it has an explicit government body and law-enforcement agencies. A society, in contrast, is informally ruled, largely by conventions; it has no explicit laws and no specific ways of enforcing what laws there are except by general public pressure. The state is a comparatively recent invention. Although we did have states some time back, they were on a rather small scale. The modern state with its close interplay with the worlds of business, technology, and engineering, with its multiple relationship with other states throughout the world, is comparatively new.

JONATHAN: The answer is perhaps too general, even assuming we can so facilely distinguish law and pressure, formal structure and informal convention (matters for later discussion perhaps). We should focus on what defines a particular political entity. In the past, such an entity was called a city-state. Today it is a nation. What defines a nation? What is needed for a political unit, in addition to those items which can be identified as national, such as a common language? How do you define a political entity?

PAUL: That's what I thought I just did! What is peculiar to the state, in contrast with a nation or society, is its explicit formulation of laws.

JONATHAN: Without objecting to such an overly legalistic and perhaps impractical definition, let me merely press for a precise definition as to this structuring. What is a political nation as opposed to a cultural nation? The Polish nation, I suppose, is of longer duration than the Polish state, for example.

PAUL: A nation is a body of people sharing the same traditions and ideology; it usually has a common language or a few common languages and a common set of conventional practices. But a state has an explicit body of laws and a separate government with its own machinery in relation to which the people are supposed to function while, at the same time, they also are part of the nation.

JONATHAN: Would your definition include tribes as a nation, if they have a tribal council?

PAUL: A tribe is usually smaller than a nation. We think of a nation as covering many more people than those who are bound together in a tribe.

JONATHAN: Some tribes are bigger than some nations.

PAUL: A very large tribe is indistinguishable from a nation. The Iroquois, weren't they sometimes called a nation?

JONATHAN: Yes.

PAUL: But tribes usually do not have a long tradition.

JONATHAN: No, I wouldn't say that.

PAUL: *Usually* they do not have a tradition going back very far, nor do they usually have a common ideology. If they do, I think it would be practically impossible to make a sharp distinction between a tribe and a nation.

JONATHAN: Let's get to a basic point. What do you believe constitutes the differences in obligation between members of a nation and members of a state? What are the differences between the obligations you have to people in a political state and those you have to people in a nation?

PAUL: In a nation our obligations essentially stem from loyalty to a conventional and inherited body of practices. Our responsibility to the state, on the other hand, is that of being "a good citizen," that is, living in accordance with the laws which define that particular state.

JONATHAN: Where does loyalty come from in the first place? I mean, why should you be loyal to someone who shares your heritage?

PAUL: Partly, I suppose, because those who share and promote your heritage have probably contributed to and assisted the very process of your growing up.

JONATHAN: Assisted or fed, you were not yet a part of the system, nor were you there by free choice.

PAUL: But you *were* protected, assisted, and fed.

JONATHAN: Not by the heritage, not by your "fellow members" of the nation living in Dubuque, if you were raised in a New York slum. When you were growing up on the lower East Side of New York, what obligation did you have to somebody in Dubuque, which stemmed from a common political state?

PAUL: The milk I was drinking, the vegetables and meat I was eating, came from all parts of the country—to which the people in Dubuque probably contributed in some way.

JONATHAN: That cuts exactly the opposite way too. For then you don't have any obligation to anybody when the vast majority of goods come from outside the country, as perhaps they do even now, here. Should little children be interested in the Japanese because most of the toys they play with are made in Japan?

PAUL: In the end, the answer would have to be yes. The bond that we have with the people in our own nation and state is only a limited one; ultimately, we ought to see ourselves as belonging to one mankind.

JONATHAN: But that doesn't answer the question. The point is, precisely why this particular loyalty to this particular nation? Why distinguish between a loyalty to mankind, a loyalty to those who indirectly aid us, and a loyalty to those in our state?

PAUL: By virtue of our common language, our common heritage, our common stories, literature, and activities, we have more in common with these members of society. We are more closely affiliated with them, we are more closely bound to them. Despite the diversity of religions in this country, for example, we share a certain religious tradition, which is a Western tradition of religion.

JONATHAN: That answer confuses me a little. I supposed the strength of this country lies in the diversity of ethnic groups and the existence of a degree of common tolerance. Would you argue that we have fewer obligations to, let's say, Hindus living in Dubuque than we do to people of a Western religious tradition living, let me say, in upper Oregon?

PAUL: So far as we belong to one mankind, we are equally obligated to all people.

JONATHAN: I'm talking about a particular loyalty in a state.

PAUL: If we were talking about a particular loyalty, I would say that greater loyalty is expected of me toward my family than toward my neighbor, greater loyalty again toward my neighbor than toward someone who lives at a distance, and greater loyalty yet again toward someone at a distance than toward someone of another nation and another country, given his different background and inheritance.

JONATHAN: Surely you must have a more subtle notion of the kinds of distances, other than mere miles, which weaken one's obligations?

PAUL: That's true. I have a loyalty toward Americans, no matter where they are, whether in China or Brazil. Loyalty is based not on proximity (although people in a nation usually live more or less close together) but on the inheritance of a common tradition and common values and ideologies.

JONATHAN: We do have some sort of common reference, I suppose, but I'm not convinced it's a common heritage. But what I want you to show me is how you make the transition from your assumption of common heritage to a particular loyalty owed to, say, Americans which you do not owe to other members of mankind. Why does that particular differentiated loyalty stem from a common heritage? Why is that?

PAUL: I think one could certainly suggest why this may be by going through a number of steps. You would recognize, I think, that Christians have some kind of responsibility toward one another which precedes their responsibility toward people of another religion; that you have some kind of responsibility to members of your own family that precedes your responsibilities to members of other families. By extension of this reasoning, would you not have a greater responsibility to members of your own nation, to your own people (which we have defined as possessing a common background, inheritance, and outlook), than you have to people who do not share that heritage and perspective? But this does not obviate the fact that we do share a common bond and destiny with all humans.

JONATHAN: Yes. I think you're touching on something crucial now. I think that Locke and Hobbes and all the other philosophers who believed there is a "social contract" had the right impulse, if the wrong formulation. Instead of declaring an explicit compact, which I think mistakes analysis for history, I would say that we may recognize an implicit contractual relationship which is somehow suggested or implied by what you call common heritage, but which I would rather consider the assumption that we have common references. That is, I am loyal to those that I suspect will be loyal to me. There is an implicit bargain resting on common values and common institutions for living together. In the event my home is attacked, another citizen will help me in part because he believes that if his home were attacked I would help him. We are members of a system of assumed promises of mutual aid, not in terms of what we have really shared, particularly in this country I think, but rather in terms of what we can count on from others, indicated by common institutions and authorities. We have a practical loyalty which may mature into an emotional one. It is because of that loyalty, both assumed and grown into, that we have a nation that is not really founded on explicit promise. Instead, we share only a common assumption resting on governmental institutions or, sometimes, national heritage—some general reference we all recognize.

We assume that we are able to count on others and that therefore they should be able to count on us. This implicit way in which we deal with others may be seen in every aspect of our lives. When we travel, for example, we expect not to be cheated; we expect to be able to go to common arbiters of disputes. Common trust, institutions, and reliance as members of a political state, the common reference of decision, politics, and laws that draw us closer than mere society, are what I think defines the nation. If there is a "contract" at all, that's all it consists of.

PAUL: There is much I like in what you say. First of all, it seems to me you're right about the "social contract." It is, as you say, a "contract" made by the people who constitute a society. I think, too, you correctly emphasized the fact that the contract is implicit. The part I do not like in what you say is the supposition that we are involved in a *quid pro quo*. We are never altogether sure whether we will be helped by others. In your account of it, it seems that the social contract is somehow justified by or grounded in the awareness that we have the ability to use common governmental agencies. I don't think this is correct.

We can have a society, a nation, without a state. We can have a state without having a nation. So I don't think that we can really identify the social contract in your way. And if you believe that in the United States we really can, or do, look forward to having other people help us just as much as we would be willing to help them, I believe you are being a bit optimistic.

JONATHAN: I think you brought out a point that I blurred initially. Perhaps it may have been too limiting to put the problem in terms of self-defense, in terms of getting help and being helpful. Perhaps I should have said that we count on other people to augment what is rich in our lives as well as to assist and defend us when we are in trouble. To put it only in terms of self-defense is too narrow. I think that you caught what I had left out; that is, that the purpose is personal and cultural enhancement. To deny this is to blur a distinction made earlier between nations and society. There are different types and intensities of this which allow certain powers and resources that we should use for the good of all men and for our personal fulfillment. These ties giving us these resources obligate us to those to whom we are tied. But I must add it is not the existence of formal laws that grounds our identity as a nation, but an expectation of loyalty and commonality, expressed and reinforced by the existence of and recourse to common patterns and institutions found in the state.

PAUL: You are quite right.

JONATHAN: I'm trying to focus particularly on our loyalty to other members of the nation. This loyalty exists, I think, by reference to a common institution which helps us live together in a distinctive way defined somehow by these political institutions rather than by our cultural heritage. But I would say that you were right to object to what I left out, that is, that the function of these political institutions does in fact contribute to the fulfillment of our roles as members of mankind—and also as members of a society of which our nation may be no more than a subdivision.

PAUL: Yes, but I don't think you have altogether faced the idea that a nation need not be subordinate to a state, that it can exist apart from a state. We cannot therefore define the loyalty of the members of a nation to one another in terms of the capacity to evoke common governmental bodies to protect or even to augment their lives. We have to understand that there is such a thing as nonpolitical loyalty, which I think does arise out of a shared inheritance and a common outlook; from having similar heroes, some great common holidays, a common language with its common nouns and emphases and pejorative and honorific terms; from participating through that common language and those shared beliefs in the creation and perpetuation of a common outlook and sense of values; and from an identifiable attitude toward the world and toward one another.

JONATHAN: I think all that is not particularly true in a simple way for this country, since men with different ethnic, philosophical, and aesthetic backgrounds live here with identical political loyalties.

PAUL: I am using three categories, whereas I think you are using only two. I would distinguish society, a nation, and a state. A "political nation" is actually a state and not a nation at all. The nation has no political structure. If we do not make this distinction, we are going to confuse the existence of a stable body of men who have a common history and common outlook with the fact that that same body can be ruled by people who do not belong to it. A nation can be governed by an alien state, but no nation is alien to the people that constitute it.

JONATHAN: I think I would agree with what you are saying, but I do not see how it establishes a distinction. Even when people are governed by men whose ideas and impulses are alien to them, they will look to this governing body and obey its laws. Bad leaders have an imperfect state. How this changes our political and general relationships to other members of society, when it diminishes our loyalty, is a very difficult question. It is not merely history which defines a nation, for other ties are relevant, and political ties make a political state. Also I would say that when you analyze a nation in terms of a common heritage you are mistaking history for analysis.

PAUL: I don't agree. The nation lives its history every day. The holidays commemorate it.

JONATHAN: Can you name a national holiday in this country?

PAUL: The Fourth of July.

JONATHAN: The Fourth of July is set by state legislatures.

PAUL: That may be the case, but doesn't the post office close on the Fourth of July?

JONATHAN: There are holidays the federal government recognizes that some states do not recognize. There are holidays recognized by some states that are not recognized by the federal government. The Alabama state capitol, for example, does not fly the United States flag.

PAUL: But isn't the Fourth of July a holiday on which all government offices are closed and all government functions cease? In that sense I would say that it is a national holiday.

JONATHAN: Insofar as it is celebrated across the whole nation, I suppose you could call it national, but it is certainly not celebrated by the entire population.

PAUL: That's true.

JONATHAN: And certainly you can find holidays that are celebrated intensely in some parts of the country but held in contempt in others.

PAUL: That's also true. Therefore we should say that they are not national holidays.

JONATHAN: Let's return to the problem of making distinctions. You seem to think alien leaders can be distinguished from not so alien leaders or from leaders who in some sense embody the spirit of the people. I would say that all of us respond in some manner to the government and that there is a subtle gradation in the "goodness" of the government or in the degree of people's response to it rather than a clear-cut distinction between alien and non-alien, or good and bad. If people look to a common government for support, I think a political state exists.

PAUL: There are tyrannies and always have been tyrannies in which states and their laws have been imposed on a people. The people have sometimes opposed them instead of looking to them for support.

JONATHAN: But I think that every government is a tyranny insofar as it applies sanctions. In some degree, all laws are opposed.

PAUL: A whole *nation* may be opposed to these laws and look for the overthrow of the *state*.

JONATHAN: If the whole nation were opposed, there would only be one man in the government.

PAUL: When MacArthur went to Japan, he imposed an alien government on the Japanese and did not in any sense become part of the Japanese nation. Indeed, he opposed some of their basic national attitudes and made them divest themselves of their religious ties with the emperor.

JONATHAN: MacArthur is both a good and an extreme example. However, I think MacArthur cannot be used as an example of a man who imposed alien measures to which men nevertheless responded. MacArthur instituted many reforms that the Japanese had written about before he went there. Many Japanese were happy to accede to what he wanted, and in fact when he left, they continued, perhaps unwisely, many of his measures.

PAUL: Nevertheless, he went there as a conqueror and imposed upon the Japanese a state which was not in accord with their national outlook.

JONATHAN: Even conquerors to some degree embody the national outlook of the conquered people because they speak their language and use some of their officials. For example, in Germany some Nazis were put back in power immediately after the war, because we felt we needed them to establish a government. No government is totally alien to a people, because it has to use the language, the tradition—even the buildings of that people.

PAUL: Then, according to that, there are really no alien conquerors.

JONATHAN: Oh, no, no, of course there are. The amount of opposition is a matter of degree. For example, in elections in this country, we try in some sense to overthrow the government. In other countries we try to overthrow the conquerors. In both cases we try to overthrow them because they impose what we do not like, but in the case of tyrannies we abhor what they impose in some more basic sense.

PAUL: But suppose the bureaucracy of a government was made up entirely of the conqueror and sycophants who in no way responded to the interests or the desires and traditions of the people who were being ruled.

JONATHAN: In no way at all?

PAUL: In no way at all. The people would then in fact be slaves. This I think happened when the Spanish and the Portuguese conquered South America. They made the Indians a subject people. When England took over India, it allied itself with certain minority groups, the Moslems and the Parsis, in order to keep the majority, the Hindus, in subjection.

JONATHAN: When you introduce slavery, you introduce a point

which I suppose ought to be considered, although it does not dispose of the issue. For a nation to exist, some degree of mobility and freedom is necessary. If a man is chained to a farm, unable to move, dependent on someone above him for everything he needs, then although he is a man, he is not a member of the community. He participates in the nation through somebody else. He can be a member of a subculture and his striving can have meaning, but he is not really a member of society. He can look to nobody at all.

PAUL: I don't agree with that; I think the nation can be made up of many subcultures. Cultures of a subordinate group help constitute the character of the total outlook; the fact that a man is a slave or has no voice in the determination of general principles does not preclude his being part of a culture and contributing to the nation as a whole.

JONATHAN: Perhaps this issue of slavery can bring us to a discussion of political jargon and debate. There are three words we hear often. One is capitalism; another is communism; the third is democracy. The capitalists say that democracy and capitalism are more or less synonymous. The communists say they are the true democrats. Would you like to start by essaying a definition of each of these?

PAUL: Capitalism defines an economic system primarily; democracy and communism define political systems. Economic systems and political systems are not necessarily separable, but they are certainly analytically distinct. Democracy stresses the preservation of certain civil and possibly natural rights; it thinks the best way to preserve these is to allow a loose form of organization. It is willing to sacrifice efficiency in order to protect these values. Communism professes the very same objectives. Communists say that their state will eventually wither away, that their object is to attain maximum peace and prosperity. They think the ideal procedure is to strengthen the state now in order to achieve maximum efficiency and therefore speed in attaining the final result, even at the price of sacrificing various civil and natural rights.

JONATHAN: Of course, you're talking about the existing Soviet communists rather than the propositions of Marxist doctrine.

PAUL: Right. We must not overlook the fact that both democracy and communism are means to an end. The problem of choosing between them is the problem of evaluating which is the better means. Do we want an inefficient system which preserves in the present some of the things we want at the end, or do we want a system that is presumably efficient but is willing to make sacrifices so that the final end can be more readily achieved? I think that an intelligent defense can be made for the communist side; I prefer the democratic answer myself because I think the people who are living today are as entitled to their happiness and freedom as the people who will live after them. Capitalism is, I suppose, associated with free enterprise, though we must not overlook the fact that monopoly and government regulation exist. I think capitalism exists as long as business has a certain degree of autonomy. Not just in Russia, but in France and Italy as well, business is controlled by the central government. In this sense the Soviet system should not be compared to capitalist systems but to those systems where business, particularly big business, has a certain degree of freedom or autonomy. Capitalism exists in France and Italy, but it is subject to stronger governmental control than it is in the United States.

JONATHAN: I'm not totally sure I agree with your account, but let me ask you a question. Do you think that capitalism is good for democracy or incompatible with democracy? There is an argument, harking back to our discussion of contract, that if people are free to contract about their business relations this economic freedom and mobility gives them a basic autonomy to move so that they can then establish their political institutions. But money also allows people to buy power and with power you can buy oppression. Certainly we see this happening in this country. When General Electric and Westinghouse were caught fixing prices, they were fined substantially; they had to pay triple damages. When they came to pay their taxes, however, because of their political influence they were allowed to deduct as a legal business expense all the money they had paid in fines. In a sense the government and the taxpayer subsidized General Electric's and Westinghouse's dishonesty. We can multiply this with example after example.

PAUL: I agree that if capitalism is uncontrolled—and we understand by a capitalistic country one in which big-businessmen are free of government supervision and control —we will go counter to democracy by not protecting people's ultimate civil and I think natural rights. Capitalism inside a democracy must be understood as controlled freedom to adventure in business. So far as this control is thought by many people to define socialism, I would say that we in this country have a socialistic government. The difference between ours and Russia's is not very great. In this sense I think that the rightists in this country, the Birchites and others, are correct in their analysis. They are wrong, however, in wanting us to go back to a free-enterprise, capitalistic system, for the reasons that you have pointed out and for related reasons.

JONATHAN: What perturbs some of us, however, is that perhaps there is something in capitalism that is inherently incompatible with democracy. Let me put it this way. Perhaps when we give people freedom to amass money, they accumulate so much that they corrupt the institutions that should control them.

PAUL: I agree with that.

JONATHAN: Let me go on. The cliché that one hears about administrative law is that regulative agencies are regulated by those they are trying to regulate. In the case of railroads or public utilities, we have the worst of both worlds. Useless competition or monopoly profits continue, yet at the same time there is parallel bureaucracy such as would exist with state ownership. Facilities are duplicated but there is no control of monopolistic power.

PAUL: I think some controls are quite effective—for example, control of airplanes, the airlines, and the air lanes. I think also that government control has fallen down in many respects—for example, in the pure food and drug acts. Yet, though we see great violations and failures in those areas, the controls are on the whole successful. This country is a much healthier country than it was fifty or seventy years ago when these controls were not in existence. If you mean by capitalism no control at all, then capitalism is inconsistent with democracy. But if you mean that some kind of government control is exercised but that nevertheless business is allowed the freedom to make a profit, then democracy and capitalism are compatible.

JONATHAN: But this does not answer the point that I have made, and I question your facts. Take as the clearest example what I would call necessary monopolies. Telephones are one example, railroads another. Parenthetically, I don't think your airplane-industry example is a good one. First, the industry is relatively young. Second, it is not entirely successful. If you have read the reports of the Civil Aeronautics Board, you will see that we've risked more accidents than other countries do; that in fact the government subsidizes a lot of badly run airlines which often do not meet their contractual obligations, e.g., chartered student flights that do not fly. Returning to necessary monopolies, we can see the phenomenal difference between our railroads and state-owned railroads abroad. Where does President Johnson look for ideas for improving the railroads? To Japan, where they are state-owned.

He wants to build a railroad from Boston to Washington that imitates the Japanese railroads. In this country we heavily subsidized the railroads when they were being built and only attempted to control them later. Consequently, our railroads are in much worse condition than those in countries with much poorer natural resources and much lower per capita income.

PAUL: Yes, but it seems to me the alternative would be a government-owned world of business and technology. Then we'd be subject to bureaucrats and autocracy and perhaps even ultimately to some kind of tyranny. I would say that the American outlook cannot be characterized as primarily either capitalistic or democratic. As you know, the authors of the Federalist Papers wanted this country to be a republic—not everyone was to have the vote. The United States is more properly termed not a democracy or a capitalist system but a pluralism where a multiplicity of different enterprises are allowed their freedom as long as they permit the freedom of one another. And the ultimate function of the government as it was originally conceived is minimal regulation in order to achieve maximal freedom. The trouble has been, as you pointed out, that certain facets of the pluralistic system become powerful, and the more powerful they become, the more necessary it is to regulate and subjugate them. We haven't succeeded altogether. I think the basic outlook in this country is that capitalism should be allowed its head only as long as it does not interfere with the commonwealth. We do not want to interfere with other kinds of freedom such as the freedom of the schools, the freedom of civil-rights movements, the freedom for general education, and ultimately the freedom of the government to enact and enforce legislation for the benefit of all.

JONATHAN: That puts it quite aptly, but I would still insist upon a couple of points and problems. One problem that bothers me is well summarized in the recent book by Estes Kefauver about business practices. I am not sure that the assumption that we can control facets of the system when they become too powerful isn't locking the barn door after the horse is gone. I think monopoly is too big to allow private citizens or often even the government to control it. Regulation after the fact may do some good, but the fact that it does some good may keep people from realizing that other measures could accomplish more. I would like to see all natural monopolies controlled by non-profit organizations related to the government but separated from it. But even if we were to control natural monopolies, what troubles many people is that the untrammeled pursuit of money may allow companies to become as big as if they were natural monopolies. We see the impact that General Motors can have on the economy. My feeling is that companies do not have to be that big. If they are, it is a fault of the culture, which has as its ostensible main ends the acquisition of goods, money, and political power. The system, of course, feeds on itself as those in power teach that they represent the good. When people are differently oriented so that they see the other goals of civilization, then, like you, I would support initial capitalistic freedom to contract and invest. If in fact people are oriented and educated properly, if there are no large gifts of economic power, and if there is a free press and a constitution guaranteeing rights, then we can allow commercial adventures. The dangers of capitalism are in the gifts of natural monopolies to a few, and the allowing of bigness until it is too late to control. Without an explicit focus on the aims of civilization, democracy may be threatened by capitalism. And I suggest that starting with complete freedom to amass power may end with powerful people under no control abusing the rights of others.

PAUL: In essence, we do agree. I think now we ought to examine this idea of pluralism. It applies not only to the multiple activities in which we engage, particularly in organized form, but it is also reflected in our own attitude toward immigrants and minority groups. The outstanding philosophies that we have developed in this country are essentially pluralistic. I am thinking about the philosophy of pragmatism, for example, as represented by Peirce, James, and Dewey. James in fact explicitly called his view pluralistic. There have of course been philosophers in America who have been essentially anti-pluralistic, but even they have recognized the existence of multiple strands each of which deserves independent consideration and all of which have to be integrated to give a final, single, unitary outlook. I think also that the very structure of the United States is another indication of our characteristic pluralism. We have not only the United States of America as a single body with its own law and president; we also have our fifty states with their separate governments and separate laws and courts. Of course, part of the problem of America is that we must adjudicate between the federal and state governments. We will never altogether get rid of the semi-autonomy of the individual states, nor ought we to, so long as we want to live in consonance with our inheritance, which consists of a basic pluralism on every front.

JONATHAN: Let me see if I understand you. I would say that in terms of their fundamental importance there is not necessarily a distinction between what you call pluralism and what you call democracy. The function of pluralism, if I understand your definition, is to preserve certain types of freedoms and the possibility of future growth. I would say democracy rests upon the assumption in political life that today's minority might be tomorrow's majority. Constitutional democracy rests on the recognition of certain rights and procedures. This recognition of certain rights and certain types of dignity rests perhaps on certain types of eternal obligations which cannot be denied. That is

why we are opposed to bigness, why we have a Bill of
Rights. Democracy itself entails a political system organized to try out new ideas. As you said, unlike communism
our goal is not the achievement of a particular end—the
achievement of an ideal state or an ideal society. We ad-
vocate democracy as a way of defining the leaders and institutions most compatible with living a civilized life and
not destroying those particular values which we establish
in a society. Therefore, democracy as I understand it is
not incompatible with pluralism, but it is not the same
system.

PAUL: I agree with what you have just said. But I think
that pluralism is a much broader way of looking at the
United States than either capitalism or democracy, because it considers multiple ways, multiple areas in which
freedom is allowed to different adventures—in our attitude toward aliens, in our philosophies, in the position
of the different states that comprise the United States, and
so on. Whereas democracy, as you pointed out, has to do
with certain basic rights, pluralism has to do with the
number of possible adventures, with allowing these to
find their way, without any control except so far as they
get in the way of one another.

JONATHAN: Conflict and clash may sometimes be good; for example,
they may help achieve accommodation.

PAUL: That's true.

JONATHAN: Would you be willing to see an American society in
which capitalism in the classic sense at least was abol-
ished?

PAUL: No, I don't see that it's necessary to abolish it.

JONATHAN: I mean, are you *willing* to see it? Would the abolition
of capitalism destroy your notion of the nature of American society?

PAUL: I don't think it's essential to American society that we
have a capitalistic system. We are moving more and more
to the position that our major, national enterprises

should be under strong government control. Our democracy is no longer what it was a hundred years ago. We have instead a kind of socialism, and this I think is a move in the right direction. I look forward to seeing Medicare applied to all people regardless of age, and I think this will happen in the next decades. We now have universal education. We will eventually move to the position that New Zealand and Sweden take with respect to health privileges for all the people.

JONATHAN: I don't think our democracy has changed. We have merely modified our gifts of economic power. However, I think our definition of what constitutes a human being may have changed. It is a cliché that what a man has a right to has changed so that it now embodies economic rights as well as political rights. But that's too neat a distinction. It's rather that we now recognize what things a man has a right to demand from the state if he is to have an equal footing with his neighbors. We recognize that a certain type of economic advantage exists.

PAUL: I think what you have said means that we have a more perceptive or penetrating grasp of the nature, needs, and promises of men. We recognize certain rights that were denied men in the past.

JONATHAN: The next question I have is this: what part of Russian communism as we have discussed it would you say is incompatible with your notion of pluralism?

PAUL: That's an excellent question. First of all, as you know, the Russians think of themselves as a Soviet or a combination of independent nations. They emphasize the fact that they are doing a great deal to preserve the nationhood, the languages, the traditions, the values, and the customs of their subordinate republics. In this sense they are radically pluralistic. Nevertheless, there is in Russia a monolithic character to the central government. Although in the United States the federal government does dominate the fifty state governments, this domination is the product of slow-moving decisions by the courts. I would expect in the course of time that the Russian and the American experiments will not deviate from each other as much as they do now, but even with the mono- lithic character of the Russian state, which defines what the subordinate parts can do, and even with the kinds of restriction to which it subjects its business and its citizens, the two countries are not now so very different. They both want to achieve peace and prosperity for all their people. Both of them are narrow in that they are not concerned with all mankind but only with a segment of it. Although they claim occasionally that they will defend other peo- ples, we know that as a rule those they defend are those who share their ideology and can be in some sense allied with them commercially and politically.

JONATHAN: We've now handled three abstract issues. The first is the nature of the state. The second is the loyalty of the individuals in the state. The third is the three traditional categories common in debates of the day. Let's now dis- cuss more concrete issues. For example, what is a man's obligation to participate in a political state? Let's start with a simple question. We know if you live in a state like New York State your vote in a presidential election does not mean anything at all. Should you vote?

PAUL: Instead of answering that question directly, may I point up its difficulties by reference to a recent occurrence? The President of the United States invited a number of dis- tinguished writers—poets, dramatists, and novelists—to go to Washington. Mr. Saul Bellow, a fine novelist and re- cent winner of the Pulitzer Prize, said at this meeting that a novelist is not a political figure and that though he dis- agreed with the President's policy in Vietnam he neverthe- less wanted to acknowledge the President's good will to- ward the arts. Mr. Robert Lowell, a very distinguished —perhaps our most distinguished—poet, wrote a letter to the President saying that though he agreed with the Presi-

dent's domestic policies he was so strongly opposed to his
foreign policies that he felt he was unable to attend. I
think that it is possible for both men to be right despite
the fact that one felt he couldn't go to Washington and
the other felt he could. An artist can by expressing himself through a gesture point up a great injustice. It was
good for Robert Lowell to make a gesture indicating that
he was aware of a grave injustice. But it would have been
much better if, instead of writing the letter, he had written a poem which would make clear what the injustice
was. To get back to the question you asked me originally,
I would say that many people should not involve themselves in politics. I'm thinking of creative thinkers, creative workers, and religious men whose orientation is elsewhere. This does not mean that they must be blind to the
failures of the political world. In the face of those failures
they must express themselves, but I think they do this best
inside their own particular competence.

JONATHAN: I approach both problems from a different angle. First,
to twist the old cliché, I believe that with power comes
responsibility. Second, for the reasons we pointed out
earlier, I believe some obligations for all mature men,
poets or not, arise because they were nurtured by the
state. But I do not think that means that Lowell should
write a poem. A poet should write a poem if he feels like
writing a poem. He is not obligated to express his political views in poetry. On the other hand, when he's dealing
with politics he should do that in the most effective way.
In fact, if I'm not mistaken, this is roughly the view you
set forth in *The World of Art*.

PAUL: I am not saying that Lowell should sit down and write
a poem for the occasion. I think it's right for him to make
some gesture indicating what he thinks is a serious failure
on the part of the government, but I would say it would
be best for him, and for all of us, if the gesture could
take the shape of a poem. If he feels so deeply about Viet-

nam, I should think that this would be close to the source of his creative powers. If he cannot write the poem, I wouldn't make him do it.

JONATHAN: I would still say that when he speaks in the political realm he should speak in the most effective way, and a poem is probably not the most effective way.

PAUL: Perhaps it is for him.

JONATHAN: No, in the political area I suppose we are more interested in impact than in personal fulfillment. He has the ability to speak effectively because of his fame; his letter would reach far more people than his published poem.

PAUL: I didn't object to his writing a letter of refusal, but there is no reason why he couldn't have written that letter and also have gone. I think there is something that Saul Bellow saw that Robert Lowell did not see. The President of the United States, as a representative of the people, was acknowledging the importance of art in our civilization. And having written a letter making clear how he disagreed with the President, I think Lowell in good conscience could have gone to the party.

JONATHAN: I agree he could have gone in good conscience but not with as much effect. I think he was after the effect.

PAUL: Then I would say he was functioning as a political figure, and he should not.

JONATHAN: No, that's where I think we disagree. As I said, with power comes responsibility, but people, through no fault of their own, achieve power without being prepared for responsibility. A man who has sat down and mastered the field of poetry becomes a person we look to for some guidance. He may not be able to give us that guidance just because he sat down and separated himself from the world where people do give guidance. That is to say, this man may become a leader because he has mastered a discipline. People then look to him for guidance in other disciplines, particularly in the public world. Now, although I think we would both agree that to master one discipline is to have an insight into all the related disciplines, this still doesn't give you the practical sophistication necessary in political fields. So what does such a leader do? If he is mature and understands what the problem is, he may keep quiet, or speak in terms of his own discipline, or if he thinks he understands the political problem, speak as effectively and as accurately as he can. It would seem to me that Lowell had power thrust upon him. He thought he was as wise as the politicians, and therefore when he refused to go he made his gesture acting as a politician. But the problem is a general one. What do you do when you have power thrust upon you? This is similar to the question I was asking earlier: what do you do when you have responsibilities thrust upon you? What is your obligation to participate? Should I then vote when I'm not informed? Should I vote at all when it makes no difference?

PAUL: There are a number of questions tied together here. We have certain minimal obligations as members of society, nation, and state. The last involves the obligation to engage in responsible voting. But after we have exercised our minimal responsibilities of good citizenship there are multiple activities and kinds of lives we can lead of which only one is political. The supposition that the political subtends all of them, that all of us somehow must utilize the powers and the reputation that we have in order to involve ourselves in political affairs, I would reject. Although Robert Lowell has the right, even the duty, as an individual citizen and a man of distinction to express his attitude toward what he thinks are failures on the part of political leaders, I think he ought not to confuse this decision with a political action as expressed in a refusal to attend a non-political reception given by the President in order to honor the arts.

JONATHAN: I'm not sure the President is ever non-political, but let's leave this dispute to return to the particular problem of voting. As I said before, it's a nuisance to vote. It's difficult to vote. It takes some time. If it has no impact, why should you vote?

PAUL: It has some kind of an effect. Sometimes the lines are fairly well drawn. In the contest between Johnson and Goldwater there were definite issues, and the choice is now bearing fruit in the sense that Medicare, of which Goldwater did not approve, now exists.

JONATHAN: But it's not just a question of whether real issues are present; your vote has no impact.

PAUL: No individual impact, but we add up the units and they make a quantity that dictates the difference.

JONATHAN: Why should I vote in New York for Johnson if Johnson's going to win by a large majority?

PAUL: The large majority is made up by people who know that Johnson's going to win, and if every one of them said, "Well, because we know he's going to win, we're not going to vote," he would lose. That's what happened when all the polls seemed to show that Dewey was ahead of Truman. Many people relaxed because they thought Dewey was going to be elected. Many other people—I was one of them—became afraid that Dewey would be elected and went to the polls to vote for Truman. We cannot deny that we are only one of millions, but all the ones add up to those millions. That is the way individuals function in a democracy.

JONATHAN: I just don't think that argument gets you far in terms of practical judgment. That is, if you yourself hadn't voted, it would have made practically no difference. Is that not true?

PAUL: As an individual, yes.

JONATHAN: Why then as an individual should you have voted?

PAUL: Because the quantity that determines the election is made up of such individuals as I, and therefore I can contribute my one millionth or my one fifty millionth.

JONATHAN: Why is it worth doing, seeing how little it is, and how much effort it costs?

PAUL: Because, even if I am only one fifty millionth of a totality, I contribute my unit value.

JONATHAN: My own feeling is that the unit value is not enough. I would, however, make another argument, namely that you are obligated to participate to realize who you are. When I engaged in a voter-registration drive in North Carolina, what was impressive for me was the fact that the Negroes who achieved their vote felt they were more fully citizens, even though in my opinion their vote gave them very little power. When we vote, we affirm for ourselves and for society in one sense, that we are members of the society. It is a symbolic gesture almost more than anything else to affirm our participation in a democracy, rather than a rational decision based on the belief that we will be effective.

PAUL: I think your argument is sound, and perhaps makes a better point than I made.

JONATHAN: Also I think a practical result of voting is that you tend to become more involved. You tend to do things which may have a broader effect—to argue with your neighbors, to read books, to try to persuade, and so on. Turning now to the question of effective participation, or of being involved in society, what do you think of the value and meaning of civil disobedience, both as a way of participating in society and as a form of protest? I have in mind of course two particular, concrete examples which I think it may be necessary to distinguish for the purpose of our argument. First is conscientious objection to military service. Second is civil disobedience as a protest in situations where the laws may or may not be oppressive.

PAUL: I think we have to distinguish protest in the form of political action from protest in the form of non-political action. They are very often confused. Many a pacifist or conscientious objector defends his position on the grounds that it is the most effective way of achieving the final goal of democracy or civilization. But if we have a conflict of strategies it is difficult to know how to adjudicate them. The man who engages in civil disobedience is no surer than the man who engages in war that his is the better strategy for attaining their common ends. Civil disobedience, pacifism, and the like are more strongly defended on the ground that the very nature of man—his rights, his dignity, and his ultimate values—requires that he not participate in destructive activities.

JONATHAN: Perhaps you could call it not "non-political action" but individual insistence.

PAUL: I think you could. There are values and ideals and ends and even realities which transcend the purview of the political order, and a man can excuse himself from participation in warlike activities because of them. We grant this today, but within a very limited domain—religion. I think a man should be privileged to say that he does not want to participate in a war because he is a painter or because he is a speculative thinker or because he is a novelist, or because he is occupied with sustaining basic ethical principles, not just because he is religious.

JONATHAN: What about a man who says he doesn't want to go to war because he's a truck driver and enjoys his work, or because he loves his children, or because he's scared of dying?

PAUL: These we presume are the common denominators of all men and therefore they offer no differentiating factor.

JONATHAN: Truck driving is not a common denominator.

PAUL: No, the common denominator is that the man likes his job.

JONATHAN: I would say that is a rare occurrence.

PAUL: I think that enough people like their jobs to make it insufficient grounds for refusal to go to war.

JONATHAN: A creative thinker may like his job of creative thinking.

Perhaps he should go and suffer because he owes society his pleasure, whereas a truck driver should be exempt because society owes him for his pain if he does not enjoy his job.

PAUL: Creative thinking is not a job. What a creative thinker is doing is cherishing and pursuing certain values which are quite different from those that interest the state. The truck driver is part of the commercial world, which is inseparable from the creation and utilization of material means in order to enable mankind to inch its way toward ultimate peace.

JONATHAN: I hope you are not doing what you appear to be doing; that is, denying the essential equality of men.

PAUL: I hope I'm not doing that either.

JONATHAN: But you are saying that people have different roles to perform.

PAUL: That's right.

JONATHAN: I'm afraid your argument would work out to deny basic equality in practice. I don't want to give anybody the power to judge roles in society or to judge their contribution to ultimately civilized values. It's a very idealistic, utopian sort of idea which would be open to terrible abuse.

PAUL: But when people say they have religious convictions we see if they are affiliated with churches.

JONATHAN: There are serious troubles with that procedure.

PAUL: It does not work out as well as it should; but on the whole we act with justice.

JONATHAN: I am not sure of that and certainly where it fails, it produces an injustice.

PAUL: I don't see why it cannot be made to work with more justice. I don't know why we can't establish criteria that would testify to whether a man is a really creative, serious artist.

JONATHAN: We can't because the administrative mind is incapable of such adjudication, leaving aside the snobbery of such an exemption and the cultivation of orthodox positions as favored.

PAUL: I don't know that it's incapable. It may find the job difficult, but I wonder if it would find it impossible. I think my earlier statement on the draft did sound like snobbism, as if a low order of people were to be drafted and others were to be freed from the draft because of their noble outlook. I was not intending this. The political dimension is only one dimension alongside others; these others have just as much right to be and to develop as the political; there are joys and rewards in the political dimension; there also are elements of difficulty, failure, and defeat in non-political enterprises. I am not urging that certain people be freed from something onerous and disgusting and horrible and dangerous in order to lead a free and more or less empty life. On the contrary, I am urging once again the pluralistic thesis that rights should be accorded to enterprises other than the political or the military.

JONATHAN: Three possible objections might be made to your position. First, to have a warrior class, we may need more people than we have; second, participation in war may help all men to understand themselves and what it means to belong to society; and third, insofar as we are obligated to help each other, one of the obligations that always follows is participation in military service.

PAUL: I think those are three very strong points. But perhaps if I answered the third my answer would take care of the other two. Participation in a basic enterprise of man which is not political is also a way of helping mankind.

JONATHAN: But I thought we recognized we had obligations to society which are not obligations to mankind.

PAUL: I can also help society by turning my back on it. It's a strange and interesting phenomenon that many things are achieved not by attending to them directly but by attending to something else. Great gains in civilization have been achieved by men who thought of themselves not as contributing to civilization but as contributing to architecture or to sculpture or to drama or to philosophy or to history.

JONATHAN: Without a doubt, but perhaps the political furnished the necessary conditions for these enterprises.

PAUL: Perhaps. Certainly, we do need government to help us live a more or less peaceful life, to protect respectable citizens against vandals, thieves, and maniacs.

JONATHAN: I suspect that the remark you made earlier about democracy versus communism is relevant here too—that telling someone to abandon his artistic life to preserve the future for other artists violates democratic values. It means abandoning present goods for the possibility for future goods. But such may be said of all who have meaning in life beyond politics or more narrowly, beyond the army. My own feeling is that calling to war, involving as it does death, is beyond an implicit or explicit social compact, and that forcing a man to participate in killing and risk death is so extreme we should honor refusals of those on whom such enforced service would wreak damage, and, that we should encourage their refusal as dissent in democratic society. Exemption should be based on the quality of a man's resistance to service rather than on his role in society.

PAUL: I agree with the last observation.

JONATHAN: One more question remains to be discussed and that is civil disobedience as a form of political action. One can make a better case for it than for voting since it shows direct involvement in the political machinery. Are you in favor of or opposed to civil disobedience as an effective form of protest, or do you think it depends on the particular circumstances? Do you think Thoreau was a stupid, an ill-advised, or a good man? Do you think that, considering conditions in the South, people should sit in and be arrested? Do you think Martin Luther King is good, or do you think that Malcolm X, who spoke violence but did not march in the streets, was preferable?

PAUL: This is an even harder set of questions than the last. I think political disobedience is, as it says, disobedience. It's a violation of the law and should be punished.

JONATHAN: It may not be a violation of the law in general. You can violate a law which, though on the books, is unconstitutional, which makes the issue a little more difficult.

PAUL: No, because it is not known to be unconstitutional until it's decided to be so by the courts.

JONATHAN: But I can show you laws that are patently unconstitutional.

PAUL: I don't see that we can call any law unconstitutional until the justices of the Supreme Court declare it unconstitutional. If you say that a law is unconstitutional and that you are going to disobey it, you must take the risk of being arrested, legitimately arrested.

JONATHAN: You hold Marshall's doctrine—that final decisions as to the constitutionality of laws should be made by judicial review, not legislative action—in the extreme. In fact, the problem is more difficult because the only way you can ever prove a law unconstitutional is to have somebody disobey it following the belief that it is unconstitutional.

PAUL: I understand that, but I say, when you disobey a law because you believe it is unconstitutional, you must also take the punishment which goes with having violated the law. Men may be willing to be punished by the civil authorities as a strategy for improving the political structure. It is an extreme form which in my opinion shouldn't be indulged in unless we are certain that all other ways are much more ineffective; it encourages the violation of the law. Aristotle long ago said men should obey even bad laws because the habit of obeying laws is an important political virtue.

JONATHAN: Would you make no distinction between three types of civil disobedience? The first is the testing of a law which is designed to oppress a particular class, say, for example, the law involving segregation and which can only be tested by "disobedience"; the second is the protesting of such a law by breaking another law—for example, some people lay down in the middle of a street in Washington to protest the segregation law; and the third are the acts of violence and destruction that occurred in the riots of long hot summers of civil rights.

PAUL: I think they are different in degree, and of course I deplore the third more than I do the other two. But insofar as the other two are violations of the law, I would say they should not be engaged in unless one is quite confident that any other device for altering the law, for moving toward justice, is bound to fail. In short, if civil disobedience is the only recourse, then in order to achieve the desired result we can engage in it. If there are other means, they ought to be used instead.

JONATHAN: In a later chapter we will discuss the nature of law, but let me just say in closing that I think it is legitimate to oppose a law when you have good reason to believe it is not a law. That is one form of political action which I would not condemn at all. The breaking of a law of the second kind, a law which we obey at other times, is an act I would condemn, unless, as you pointed out, it is the only form of effective protest. The third I view as a variant of the second and say it is condemnable only insofar as it destroys those things we do not want destroyed. Then, it seems to me, little justifies the act.

4

Society

This dialogue begins with an examination of the nature of civilization, the fact that all men are members of one mankind, and the fact that obligations follow from this. In an attempt to determine just what a civilization is, the discussants sharpen their disagreement on the nature of leaders and creativity in politics and art. From there, the discussion moves on to discuss the justification of trials of leaders of defeated nations, such as that conducted at Nuremberg. Attention is then drawn to the poverty program, the situation of the underprivileged, the Negro problem, and the meaning of misery in the world.

Paul Weiss takes the position that all men are to be seen as belonging to one mankind and all owe an obliga-

tion to all. Jonathan Weiss defines the obligation of men in terms of the goals that all should serve. Both maintain that social institutions are inadequate to satisfy the needs of men, and that men have obligations to one another beyond those which the state and other public institutions insist that they have.

JONATHAN: In the three previous chapters we have discussed various problems connected with men as individuals, men in the family, and men in the political state. We are all to some degree members of a broader community, that is, of all mankind. As was indicated, there may be differences between society and nations. At this point it is perhaps wise to consider what it means to be a member of mankind. What is the meaning of culture? What is the nature of society? What is the purpose of being a man among men?

PAUL: I think that we can recognize mankind as having at least two basic meanings. One is biological: mankind is made up of persons who can interbreed. This sense of mankind is at the root of medicine, of biology, and of the basic theories of sociology. But there is another meaning of mankind that has to do with what man's primary destiny is. In this second sense we think of mankind in terms of a possible common goal based upon spiritual elements.

JONATHAN: It is the second that I suppose we mean when we say society.

PAUL: No, because mankind may not form a single society. There can be a plurality of societies sharing in a single civilized totality which embraces all human beings. This totality is what I mean by mankind in the second sense.

JONATHAN: What claim would you say a man has on another man just by virtue of the fact that they are men?

PAUL: Because they are part of the same mankind, because

they require one another to achieve maximum protection and value, and because they all depend on one another to attain their fullest selves.

JONATHAN: Surely you don't mean that an African witch doctor and I need each other?

PAUL: Yes, I do. The witch doctor is pursuing, according to certain conventions, medical practices that are grounded in past experience. I suppose he acts in order to benefit the people of his community. To the degree that he is giving of himself for the benefit of others, he is exhibiting a spirit which you too can accept and carry out in your own particular way. Moreover, the people he benefits are presumably improved in their capacities and will be able to work with you more effectively than they could have without his efforts. You and they are forging a common civilization. Don't forget that today we do not have one common civilization embracing all mankind. We are moving toward it from a number of quite distinct bases which have very little to do with one another. So, though you may not have much direct contact with the witch doctor, you have a great deal to do with the outcome of many generations of his work with his people, just as he will have much to do with the outcome of your work in your society over the generations.

JONATHAN: Let me pose the question to you more sharply. Consider people whom I will never know. There will be two classes of these. One might be a tribe in darkest Africa who never run across anybody that I will directly or indirectly ever meet; and the second are historical entities who can have no possible dialectical relationship with me. What obligations do I owe, what connections do I have with someone from, say, the island of Atlantis?

PAUL: The problem here stems from the two meanings of mankind. Mankind in the first meaning, the biological meaning, applies to all men who have been, who now are, and who ever will be. Mankind in the second sense of a common civilization is a goal and an ideal, something which we are trying to attain. Now, presumably everybody in the past who was part of mankind was not a member of that one common civilization, but presumably they all contributed something to the eventual convergence of one single mankind.

JONATHAN: Perhaps we ought to restate the question then. What defines common civilization?

PAUL: The sharing in a common treasury of values and achievements—in the creative arts: music, drama, literature, painting, sculpture, architecture; in the sciences: physics, chemistry, biology; and in technology, which in my opinion would include engineering, business administration, economic growth. All these together make up the content of civilization. I hope that eventually all mankind will be able to contribute to that common body of knowledge, content and value, and that all men will be able to benefit from this common treasury.

JONATHAN: I suspect there is a kernel of truth in what you are saying, but as a descriptive statement I can't really accept it fully. We all belong to a number of societies, certainly. As we pointed out earlier, we are members of families, and we have different cultural heritages, racial characteristics, and economic positions. Moreover, all men are unique and individual. Each individual in Western civilization may participate in one or many of thousands of different heritages. The reason we can continue to talk about Western civilization is that there is a vantage point from which all these traditions can be seen, a common perspective rather than a common heritage.

PAUL: I think I agree with that, but I was talking about the future. I'm not sure there is even a common vision. I think there's only a convergence toward a single body of values and achievements that all men will eventually be able to participate in.

JONATHAN: No; it is not a matter of time but of nature. What I am saying is that the various heritages of Western civilization have a common perspective that suggests what it is to be a man in society. What you are saying is that somehow you wish to achieve a particular uniform goal.

PAUL: I don't think the two views are incompatible. I would agree that whatever men do, wherever they are, they express something of the nature of man. But there is also a common civilization which is made up of the achievements of Michelangelo and Bach and Dante and Shakespeare and Molière and so on. These constitute our inheritance from the past, these are the material from which we will build a more complete and complex civilization in the future.

JONATHAN: I think you are stating your point too boldly. I don't think the average person—let's say a teenager in a small town in western Pennsylvania—knows anything first hand about Michelangelo and Molière. Great ideas filter down so that even our participation in the banal is in some sense participation in the culture of the great, but to say that the average person really knows Molière or Michelangelo is wrong.

PAUL: It seems to me that what you are saying would have been more correct fifty or a hundred years ago than it is today. Because of the mass media—television, periodicals with national circulation, the movies—everybody in this country has an opportunity to become acquainted with many of the great figures and achievements of the past. I would be very much surprised if the teenager you mentioned did not have some awareness, even some knowledge, of some of the great works of the masters, if only through indirect presentation on television or through a picture in a magazine or an article in a newspaper.

JONATHAN: There is a difference between opportunity and acquaintance, and I suspect there are many who do not even have the opportunity.

PAUL: Saying that a person has a mere acquaintance is not the same thing as saying that he is really participating in that inheritance. It is very difficult to get full value out of the arts and sciences. One of the great dangers today in the proliferation of the arts and the support of the arts by the government—which I think are desirable things— is that they make people feel that the experience and enjoyment and appreciation of art, and I would say of course also of the sciences and other achievements of civilization, are quite easy. On the contrary, it is very difficult to look at a painting properly, very difficult to understand a symphony, very difficult to share in any great work of art. In this sense I think it is true that your teenager does not have a full appreciation. But it is also true of most sophisticated concertgoers, first-nighters, and museum visitors. The fact that they have these opportunities is no guarantee that they will really share in the full, rich, deep meaning of these different enterprises. But the opportunity is there, and in this sense they are more a part of one civilization than they could have been fifty or a hundred years ago.

JONATHAN: To say that in some sense the fruits of civilization are available for many people does not make the case that all men in a certain time or a certain place are members of that civilization. The way that case has to be made is to say that the very fabric of societies is defined by the great ideas being lived out by those who are being affected by them.

PAUL: I think that is ultimately an ideal to be obtained.

JONATHAN: I thought you were saying that everybody in every little hamlet should realize the import of Michelangelo.

PAUL: No, not realize the import of Michelangelo but have the opportunity to know and to appreciate it.

JONATHAN: But opportunities do not make civilization.

PAUL: I agree with that.

125

JONATHAN: You are not a member of civilization because the opportunity is presented but because the commonality has become part of daily life.

PAUL: The opportunity has been realized.

JONATHAN: But the opportunity is always realized not in the ideal sense that you are envisioning but in a more indirect, subtle, and reduced sense.

PAUL: Not "realize fully," of course.

JONATHAN: Now, the ideal of civilization is that we should all revel in the fruits of civilization.

PAUL: And contribute to it.

JONATHAN: But the reality of civilization is that the ideas and impact of the leaders filter down and become the very texture of daily living.

PAUL: Yes, but when they are the texture of daily living, they are not really of the same quality as when originally conceived. Maybe this is the point you are making. Even in the most complete fulfillment of the ideal of civilization, not all men will figure equally; there will be different grades of participation. The spirit of the leaders, those who are making the great contributions, will have to be participated in, and some of their results will have to be accepted by others who are not actually giving as much of their lives to the making and enjoyment of civilization. This is certainly true today and I think it will be true always.

JONATHAN: All right. Then let's pose the question of obligations again in this context. What do those in secondary positions owe to those in primary positions, and vice versa? What do all members of civilization owe to other members of civilization?

PAUL: This is a point with wide implications. Today civilization is made up of leaders and followers, people who break new ground and people who merely enjoy some filtered-down version of what the others have achieved.

But this will also be true when civilization's most ideal form is realized. Even then, not everybody will be making major contributions or enjoying the major contributions in the most complete possible way. There will always be people in secondary positions, but in all positions all will be equally responsible for sustaining and continuing civilization.

JONATHAN: Perhaps we are talking at different levels; you of what civilization should be, and I of what in fact defines an existing civilization.

PAUL: My point is relevant to both. Most of the time the great things that we think ought to be achieved are achieved not by directing our efforts at them but by directing our efforts at something else. To achieve civilization, we must not aim directly and fixedly at a civilized world, but at the attainment of beauty, of religious insight, of an understanding of basic ethical principles in such a way that the outcome is their exemplification in this world. If we aim at civilization, what we will eventually attain is not civilization but people sharing in it at various degrees less than the optimum. If we would like to attain civilization for all mankind, we must aim all mankind at something beyond civilization. If civilization is our horizon, then we will find that what we will obtain is multiple degrees of civilization, and this will make our civilization derivative and limited rather than ideal.

JONATHAN: Let me answer you indirectly. In the *Crito,* Socrates argued that a man should not flee the state even when he awaited death at the hands of the state. The reason was that the state had raised him, the state had defined his meaning. For him to leave the state would be a form of suicide, just as his staying to be killed by his state was certainly a form of death. As I said earlier, society is constituted by the great ideas of the great creative visions filtering down and manifesting themselves in everyday life. We participate in these creative visions, and they give us part of the meaning of our daily life. The billboards we have seen are yesterday's paintings; the clichés we hear are yesterday's poetry. To find ourselves, we must operate in a context. For example, we explain someone's behavior by saying where he came from. Many people think that to say someone holds the views he holds because he was a poor Italian or a rich white Anglo-Saxon Protestant is to explain him completely. But this isn't sufficient. A person's context gives him insight, a point of view from which to understand the world. Background does not just determine vision; it also gives insight, and I think we have an obligation to that which gives us insight. Although I think Socrates went too far in his argument about men's obligations to the state, nevertheless I think we do have an obligation to the civilization that makes the context in which we are able to manifest our vision. For this reason I say we owe greater loyalty to those who are members of our culture than we do to those who are not, although we are all striving toward what is basic and meaningful to all mankind.

PAUL: I think I agree more with the latter part of what you said than with the earlier part. Let me concentrate on the part with which I do not agree. You said the billboards of today were the paintings of yesterday, and the clichés of today the poetry of yesterday. These epigrams are rather neat, but I don't think they are really correct. There is a domain of poetry and poetic insight that has continued throughout the ages; alongside it and parallel with it is prose, which has a different objective. The primary function of prose is to communicate, to inform, and to support; whereas the primary function of poetry is to take cognizance of the weight of words, the grain of words, and the peculiar affiliations words have with one another, in order to gain an insight into ultimate reality. In this sense there is no movement from poetry to prose.

I do not see that the clichés of today are comparable with or even derivative from the poetry of yesterday, if poetry is taken to mean the imaginative language of the past. I would say further that although the design of billboards is undoubtedly influenced by what the designer has seen of great painting, it has its own rationale.

JONATHAN: I think you have interpreted what I said too literally, but let's reserve the problem of what we mean by art for a future discussion. What I was attempting to point out was that the creative efforts of cultural leaders—modified in some sense—provide the context in which we live.

PAUL: No, for that denies the independence of the people who are affected.

JONATHAN: I didn't intend any such denial.

PAUL: If you do not deny it, then you must say that the people who are being affected by the leaders have something like their own rationale and their own character, their own ideology, their own values, their own subculture.

JONATHAN: Does a disciple have his own rationale separate from his teacher?

PAUL: A mere disciple—no.

JONATHAN: Does a popularizer have a rationale separate from what he is popularizing?

PAUL: Yes. His objective is different. His rhythms are different. His way of handling things is different. The popularizer doesn't take some great work and merely spell it in another way. In trying to reach a larger audience, he shifts the meaning of the work and gives it a different kind of substance. Popularization is a transformation of a work in order that a larger public can share in some of its values.

JONATHAN: We can extract at least two abstract questions from this disagreement. The first is to determine what the purpose of the act of creation implies and what the nature of the created object is; and the second is to determine what qualifies and defines the existence of a man-made artistic object. But let's leave these questions for a future discussion and return to our initial problem. Let me pose you a very simple question: what loyalty do I owe to a member of our civilization that I do not owe to a member of mankind?

PAUL: Meaning by our civilization Western civilization in contrast to Eastern civilization?

JONATHAN: Define it as you will. I think there are ever-increasing rings of civilization both in time and in place, but if you want to define what you mean by a particular civilization or a particular range of civilizations you can describe the types of ranges of obligations that ensue because of these civilizations.

PAUL: I think we dealt with this in the last chapter. I tried to point out there the differences in our loyalty to our family, our loyalty to our society, and our loyalty to our nation. We have more significant and vital obligations toward the groups which we have been intimate with and therefore benefited from and perhaps even suffered with, than we have with respect to mankind at large.

JONATHAN: Would you include hate in this scheme? Does a Jew owe more loyalty to a German than he does to a non-German because Germans had a more powerful impact upon his culture?

PAUL: I think you have raised a very important and exciting question. Let me see if I can put it another way. Am I more intimately involved with an active Nazi than I am, say, with a peaceful, virtuous African who has never impinged on the main current of Western civilization? I think this question has two dimensions. The first is that I am obligated to and intimately involved with that Nazi as I am not with that African, not in terms of his actions but in terms of the inheritance we both respect. Even our values are shared, although we act on them in opposite ways. To use a term popular today, we are existentially closer to one another than either of us is to the African. In terms of the actual civilization of which I am a part,

I am closer to the Nazi. In terms of the ideal civilization
I wish to attain, I am closer to the African.

JONATHAN: To whom are you more obligated?

PAUL: In terms of the present "civilization," I am more obligated to the Nazi. But in terms of the civilization I would
like to attain, I am more obligated to the African. My answer depends on whether I am talking of the present or of
the achievement of the final civilization. As a philosopher,
I am closer to the African than I am to the Nazi. Were I a
politically minded man, were I a sociologist, were I a
businessman or someone concerned with preserving what
had already been produced, say a museum director, I
think I would have to say I was closer to the Nazi and
therefore more obligated to him.

JONATHAN: What would that mean in concrete terms?

PAUL: It would mean that there are certain basic things that
he and I share.

JONATHAN: No, no, what would your obligation entail? What
should you do for him?

PAUL: We would both agree to and subject ourselves to the
Geneva agreement. We would continue our diplomatic
relations via the neutral countries. We would be concerned with preserving major works of art. Even though
the Germans stole works of art from France, they tried to
preserve them.

JONATHAN: But you're talking now as a nation instead of as an individual. Consider a concrete situation. Suppose I walk
down the street with one quarter and meet two men who
both need the quarter to buy themselves a meal. Assume
I have eaten. One of the men is your African, the other
is your Nazi. Which man do I give the quarter to?

PAUL: On the basis of your illustration, I don't think you
would know the best place to put your quarter. You don't
know whether or not that quarter will teach the Nazi that
there are kind people in the world.

JONATHAN: Assume that all factors are the same except that one

131

man is your idealistic African and the other is your Nazi.

PAUL: As I just pointed out, I would find myself affiliated more with the African, who is moving toward the common ultimate civilization of us all, than with the Nazi, who is destroying part of Western civilization; in that sense it would be better to give the quarter to the African. But I can also see how someone who identified himself with existing civilization might find it better to give the quarter to the man who, though engaged in uncivilized activities, nevertheless shares the inherited values, ideology, meaning, and achievements of Western mankind.

JONATHAN: I think the purpose of civilization is to provide a concrete context in which to achieve the fruits of what it is to be creative while living with dignity. Now it is possible for a member of an existing civilization to go against his civilization's capacity to be creative, or its capacity to recognize man's dignity. I think I owe very little to those who destroy people, either directly, like the Nazis, or indirectly, like some dictators. In fact, I think they have divorced themselves from modern civilization. A man who is in favor of mankind though not a member of a closed civilization is closer to me because he has the same goals I do. Again, we are related to men through many different contexts and in many different ways. A common past is but one of them, and my loyalties may be to others who, without that common past, share my values and work for the important goals of civilization.

PAUL: Don't forget that this man with whom you are disagreeing in some ways also wants to preserve the very things that you want to preserve. Let's think further of the extreme case of the Nazi. He thinks of himself as trying to preserve the best part of mankind. He wants to destroy those parts of mankind which he thinks prevent man from achieving his maximum value. He is opposed to what he thinks is "decadent" art, not to all art. He is opposed to "decadent" music, not to all music. He is opposed to "decadent" men, not to all men. He wants to rid Western civilization of its corrosive elements. Does the fact that we disagree with him make him completely opposite to us? Like you, I find more in common with that African than I do with that Nazi, but I'm pointing out that those people who are concerned with what is practical must say that ultimately they are closer in spirit to the Nazi, even at the point where they are engaged in a bloody, relentless war with him.

JONATHAN: In some sense they do have more in common, but that does not mean they are more obligated.

PAUL: Insofar as they feel that they have more in common, they are more obligated. The Nuremberg trials were supposedly carried out according to the standards of justice that prevail in the Western world. They were to have been expressive of those very ideals which the Nazis should have themselves embodied.

JONATHAN: Let us focus on the Nuremberg trials for a moment. Were you in favor of them?

PAUL: In one way yes, because they established a precedent in terms of which we hope better trials will eventually be carried on. But in and of themselves they were not what I consider just or properly conducted legal trials.

JONATHAN: What was the good precedent?

PAUL: There are people who commit crimes against mankind whom we would like to condemn, not as victims, or as defeated enemies, but as people who have violated our common basic code. The meaning that I hope will eventually be extracted from the Nuremberg trials is that when men commit the crime of genocide they will be condemned by the rest of civilization.

JONATHAN: I believe that the Nuremberg trials were a disastrous precedent and that they made what was uniquely tragic seem almost banal. Take the second part first. In one sense, what the Nazis did was no different from what others have done before. There have been mass murders.

There has been mass racism. There have been military
states. What the Nazis did was to make a difference of
degree into a difference in nature by combining all these
evils. With what seems to me considerable success, they
defended themselves in the trials by pointing to the com-
monness of the individual evil acts. To treat the crimes
as discrete, punishable, and understandable evils was to
miss their whole meaning. The general idea that in the
heat of passion those who have won a war can judge the
leaders of another nation seems to me to go back to what
we discussed in our first chapter about wrongly assuming
a decision-making role. Once conquerors morally judge
the conquered, a propaganda-induced righteous spirit
will morally condemn victims.

PAUL: To the extent that the Nuremberg trials were merely a
continuation of the war in a legal guise, I oppose them.
But we also argued in the trials that the state is never
prior to men in the sense of having the right to subjugate
all men and deny them their fundamental right to life,
liberty, and the pursuit of happiness. And this is what
the Nazis thought in principle was correct in respect to
certain non-Aryan races; this was what the trials were
about. I agree with you that the trials were not conducted
correctly, but they do show us what we must do in the
future.

JONATHAN: You say that the actual conduct of the Nuremberg trials
was bad. What I'm saying is that trying such people as
the Nazis in a court of law will necessarily fail because a
court of law works by making particular discrete charges.
It deals with separate particular crimes. You can't try an
ideology in court because you cannot summarize the ethos
in the extremity.

PAUL: I don't think you give sufficient value to precedent. The
Magna Charta was nothing more than the result of a
struggle between the king and the barons. Neither was

concerned with the peasant. But we have all benefited from the Magna Charta because eventually the common people were acknowledged to have similar rights. Our Constitution was largely a product of the struggle between the federal government and the individual states. I suspect the Nuremberg trials will provide a precedent by which mankind will be able to stand in judgment against groups of individuals who put the state above all men and thereby deny the private, natural, and civil rights of individuals.

JONATHAN: I don't agree with your analysis. The Magna Charta did very little except limit the power of the king. Social forces did the rest. The Constitution was not the result of a struggle between the states and the United States, and its most valuable part—the Bill of Rights—was actually written after the Constitution had been passed into law. A precedent is either a case or a particular legal operation. The legal operation in the Nuremberg trials was disastrous. To let a conquering nation stand in judgment of the leaders of another nation is to claim the power to condemn on moral grounds what all people have done to some degree at other times. The Nuremberg trials condemned the Nazis for particular immoral acts rather than for their ideology. If you want to say mankind can condemn an outrageous ideology, you are right. But not by this means. The condemnation of mankind should have been expressed in a different way—particularly if it was to serve as a guide for future generations.

PAUL: I think two different meanings of precedent are being confused. You were thinking of "precedent" as a lawyer. I was using "precedent" in a common way, as an occurrence which provides a kind of guide for the future. I agree with something you are presupposing, though you haven't explicitly stated it, and that is that political organizations interact with one another in terms of power, even though they state their objectives and their ideals in terms of moral considerations. We did not go to war with the Germans because we disapproved of their behavior toward the Jews or the subject nations. All states speak to their people and to the world in terms of moral principles, but their actions are normally guided only by the desire to preserve and enhance their own power.

JONATHAN: I don't see what relevance motives have to moral judgment. Even if we attacked Japan and Germany for motives of power, we still had a right to condemn them as immoral, if they were immoral.

PAUL: I guess I didn't make myself clear. What I am trying to say is that political organizations interact with one another in terms of power; when we make a moral judgment, we are no longer speaking for a political organization but for mankind. When we went into the Nuremberg trials, although we were distinguishable as a state, we functioned as representatives of mankind. In the war we were representing only the allied states.

JONATHAN: Were we representatives of mankind or of Western civilization?

PAUL: Mankind insofar as it is attained in Western civilization.

JONATHAN: Let's leave this tangent for a minute and return to the example we started with. We've had an old argument, you and I, about whether one should give money to a beggar. Suppose we walk by a man we do not know and he asks us for a quarter. We know he's going to give that quarter to a bar or a liquor store and become drunk again. Should we give him the money?

PAUL: I would say yes. There are people in difficulty all over the world whose troubles are not eliminated by charity. Nevertheless, the fact that they are in difficulty makes them an object of charity. I give this man a quarter not in order to indulge him in his desire to drink but to rec-

ognize the fact that he has troubles which he must alleviate in his own way. I give him the money because I have
it. It is an act to help him out of the awkward situation
he is in, at least for the moment. I regret that the only
way he can solve the problems that confront him is by
getting drunk again, but the point is that I do help him
even when I let him buy more liquor.

JONATHAN: Your remarks lead to two questions. Shall I give him
the money because we are members of the same civilization? Since I cannot help every bum, why should I help
this particular bum?

PAUL: I cannot help all the people who are needy. That's why
I try to function in society as a good citizen. Presumably
I pay my taxes so that the government can distribute the
money it gets from me and others in such a way as to
benefit those people who are less fortunate than I am.
But government machinery is not perfectly efficient; I can
see all kinds of defects and limitations, and therefore
what used to be called the problem of equity confronts me.
To deal with individuals who are not altogether ac-
counted for within the ordinary government framework,
I give to private charities over and above the payments
I make to the government.

JONATHAN: But giving money to private charity is not the same
thing as giving money to a bum.

PAUL: Let's distinguish two meanings of private charity. There
is organized charity, and there is individual giving. I used
the words "private charity" in the second meaning, not
the first. Organized charity is like the government: it's
institutional. I'm distinguishing between institutional
giving and individual giving.

JONATHAN: Well, then the questions arise, why should I make individual gifts, how is that related to civilization, and,
since I cannot aid all individuals, why do we have individual giving in addition to institutional giving?

PAUL: I cannot aid all individuals without involving myself in an institution. I give to individuals because they are inadequately taken care of by institutional operations.

JONATHAN: But I cannot give to all bums. I can't even give to many bums, so why should I give to one bum?

PAUL: That is where the problem of equity comes up. When you try to deal with all bums, you need an organization, but equity concerns itself with those problems of justice which are not taken care of through institutional operations.

JONATHAN: But why should I care about equity?

PAUL: Because it is a form of justice, and as a good man you want to be just.

JONATHAN: Then should I go out of my way looking for bums?

PAUL: You are a member of civilization and of society, presumably doing significant work. If your work is not as important as the work of helping indigent, improvident, or dissolute people, then I think you should go out and help those people.

JONATHAN: Is your position that a man should be actively concerned about equity because he ought to be actively concerned about justice?

PAUL: Yes.

JONATHAN: Yet you say I should not go out of my way to find people who need help?

PAUL: Only as long as you do not have more important work to do. Justice isn't the only good in this world.

JONATHAN: In other words, it is only happenstance when you alleviate inequity?

PAUL: If I am engaged in constructive, creative work, I probably won't have the opportunity or the time to find those people who need my financial help. Therefore I use institutional channels. Should I by chance run across a case where the institution is not taking care of an individual, I function as an individual to give what I can to help that person. Now, there are other people concerned with the injustice produced by the operation of institutions, who seek out those who have suffered an injustice. As a matter of fact, you as a lawyer in Washington are doing exactly that for those people who are unable to hire private lawyers.

JONATHAN: Let's talk about that in a moment. I approach this problem from a slightly different perspective than you because it seems to me that if I do give money to a particular bum then in some sense I ought to seek out all bums. But I don't believe I should seek out bums, for just the reason that you point out—that I have more important things to do. The reason I do not refuse to give to one I confront is that not to give would be to deny who I am and what it is to be human. I am not motivated by some abstract notion of "should." To deny help to another when you confront him is to deny that you can be like that person, which is in fact to deny that you are human.

PAUL: Then why don't you go out looking for such people?

JONATHAN: Because my humanity is expressed in all the things I do. I live in a context. The context is sometimes shaped by happenstance and sometimes created. I try to do all the things I can do. When I come across a concrete situation where another human being confronts me, I must act and affirm our common humanity. My job is to live the best possible life. Some confrontations arise necessarily, some from the life I lead, some from chance. In all I must do the best I can to help others achieve dignity, and still follow my muse.

PAUL: But you could live in a nice, quiet, clean neighborhood where no intoxicated people appear on the streets, and in that way you could avoid much of what you call happenstance. You could say well, if by happenstance I run across such a person, I'll indicate my humanity, but if it never happens, then I don't have to declare my humanity.

JONATHAN: Isn't that your position?

PAUL: No. I say that when I become aware of certain cases of inequity, I take care of them.

JONATHAN: No, you don't say that. In fact, if I said go look for bums, you would say you shouldn't.

PAUL: No, I don't go look for them.

JONATHAN: There are lots of bums on the street whose pain would be eased by charity. Yet you don't go down to the Bowery every time you go to New York, and give every bum some money. Why not? You know about the inequity.

PAUL: I don't because to give to many of them is to involve myself in institutional giving. No, I give to the individual because of an awareness of the inequity that is produced by institutional giving. But I don't seek out bums because I am engaged in other kinds of activities.

JONATHAN: Then in fact your charity is a matter of happenstance.

PAUL: It is not that alone. It is also a question of ideology, whereas in your case it seems to me to depend solely on where you have placed yourself.

JONATHAN: I have placed myself where I think I can do the most good. When I encounter a human being, I do what I think I can for him. I structure my conduct in terms of my goals—and when I encounter a place where I can do some good and not weaken my general life, I do that good.

PAUL: You know there are many people who are in difficulty. Why don't you give yourself to them all the time?

JONATHAN: Mankind is in many respects a vast bleeding mass. Bums are not the only people who suffer. The middle-class man who has acquired a genteel alcoholism and comes home every night to a suburban home and drinks five martinis before supper and two drinks afterward suffers in some way. I cannot bring succor to everybody. What I try to do is find the most effective place to be.

PAUL: But wait a minute. You could reach the people in the Bowery. Why don't you?

JONATHAN: I can be more effective with more people, doing what I do. In fact, the depressed part of Washington where I work now is somewhat equivalent to the Bowery.

PAUL: You could, if you wanted to, give as much as you could spare of your weekly wages to these people. Why don't you do this? You're not clear in your principles.

JONATHAN: The answer is again a matter of effectiveness. Leaving aside the point we agree on, that I have other goals besides working for the oppressed, I lead the life I do because I feel that I can in that way most effectively help oppressed people and at the same time most effectively achieve the fruits of civilization. Within that context, when I confront people whom I can help, I do the best I can. Let me give you an example. As a lawyer I run across some clients with whom I have a real rapport, and others with whom I do not. Now for both I do all I can as a lawyer. For those with whom I have a rapport I give more than legal services. If I run across a woman who is working as a maid and is being evicted by her landlord, not only do I help keep her from being evicted but I try to get her job-training so that she can leave domestic service. And while she is in job-training I try to get her a job that will pay better wages than what she is getting. You talk as if you have some sort of abstract principle of equity, but I don't understand how it works.

PAUL: I think we have not really joined this issue. Perhaps we ought to leave it for a while and come back to it when we have clarified some fundamental ethical principles.

JONATHAN: Fine. Let's turn then to something that is in the news now and to which we have been indirectly alluding: the poverty program. I presume we both have some practical knowledge of it, although you have perhaps more theoretical knowledge. Let me explain what I mean by the poverty program. Before 1964, there were a number of acts which were designed to alleviate some aspects of poverty, for example, the Manpower Development Training Act, and the Area Redevelopment Act. These acts were designed to aid people who were not properly trained or who were depressed by conditions beyond their control. Then in 1964 we passed the Economic Opportunity Act. Its premise was that poverty could be eliminated in the United States. Under it, an agency was established to start a "war on poverty," to eradicate poverty in this country by making it possible for people who are poor through no fault of their own to get ahead. Basically, the agency tries to organize various programs to alleviate present misery and eradicate its basic causes. It is administered by contracting with various groups to establish particular programs. In practice it appears to be inefficient and full of patchwork, but with able dedicated men some valuable steps could be made. Now do you want to characterize the poverty program as you understand it and say what you think of it?

PAUL: Since you are involved in it, I have to take your characterization of it as forming the ground rules for any discussion.

JONATHAN: No, that isn't necessary. There are many different theories about the war on poverty. One theory says it is an entirely new concept. Another theory, which I somewhat favor, is that by and large it's a grab bag of useless giveaways handled by self-perpetrating bureaucrats whose mentality is alien to the poor.

PAUL: Is not the problem of poverty a problem of providing people with the instrumentality for being able to be in good health and to realize their potentialities? Solving it doesn't solve the human dilemma; it only avoids the conditions and obstacles which prevent some people from attaining their maximum status. The poverty program, therefore, only provides the means for getting somewhere —just as the civil-rights movement does.

JONATHAN: I think that is wrong, but let me go one step back and ask you what obligations we owe to the poor because we

are not poor and yet are members of the same society.
Chance has given us a better break than they.

PAUL: I think it is precisely because, by the mere accident of
birth and opportunity, or perhaps even of native gifts of
persistence and intelligence and insight, I have been ad-
vantaged, that I feel obligated to see that other people
are given the same kind of opportunity that I have been
privileged to have. Beyond that, the human being must
make himself.

JONATHAN: Of course you came out of the slums, didn't you?

PAUL: As I think of the slums today, I am inclined to say that
I came out of a shabby neighborhood, not a genuine
slum. There were no rats running around in my house.

JONATHAN: I guarantee there were.

PAUL: Not in my apartment, though; maybe in my building.
We had light in the halls and we had toilet facilities inside. We had heat, painted walls, and so on. It was an
impoverished neighborhood, but I cannot honestly say
that my neighborhood was similar to the neighborhood
where you work. I had the opportunity to get a decent
elementary education. I would say that the whole idea of
the poverty program is an extension of the meaning of
democracy: more men must be given the same opportunity to achieve a minimal exercise of rights.

JONATHAN: I think that's excellent. I think the essential question
is that of equality. Now let's approach this problem from
another angle. If you suggest that it would be better to
give every poor person ten thousand dollars and elimi-
nate all the flashy anti-poverty programs, people are
shocked and say that the poor wouldn't know how to
spend ten thousand dollars. But this sentiment is very
anti-democratic and anti-capitalistic and amounts to saying that poor people are different in nature. An upper-
middle-class person would be very happy to have ten
thousand dollars. The justification for this different treat-

ment which is close to Marxist doctrine is that the poor have been alienated from society in such a way that they're incapable of using the money to get ahead. There is some strength in that position. And if the poverty program is to have any meaning at all, its functions must be to give the poor the same power and rights as other people have to find humanity and a creativity.

PAUL: In other words, to provide them with the minimum which they have somehow been deprived of, either by virtue of birth or by circumstance, or even because of some failure, if you like, of character or discipline. We want to bring them to the position we were able to start from, and we hope that a good number of them will take advantage of this opportunity to fulfill themselves in a way that is now impossible for them to do.

JONATHAN: Perhaps the poverty program cannot work if it tries to treat people who have been warped in the ghettos for twenty-five years as if they were no different from the white middle class.

PAUL: I think that there's a good deal of truth in what you say. We're not going to be of much help to the adults in our society deprived for a long period, but our ultimate hope must be that we will do some good for the next generation and the generation beyond that. I am thinking, for example, of the problem of leisure. Leisure today is misunderstood by a great number of people, particularly by those who think of leisure as a period of recreation that enables people to go back to work with greater vigor. When people with this attitude retire from work, they find they have a great deal of idle time that has to be filled up. But genuine leisure should enable men to enrich themselves more than they could in their work. Work should be a carrying out of the great goods that have been achieved in leisure. Obviously, such a view of leisure cannot be introduced to people who have been spending forty years behind a lathe, but it can be introduced at the beginning of education. If one had such a view, one might conceivably be able to introduce an idea of leisure to the next generation that cannot now be practically significant for most adults. In this sense I agree with you entirely about the effects of twenty-five years of ghetto life.

JONATHAN: I like the idea that generations yet unborn may be less miserable. But let me return to the basic topic. The scriptures say the poor will always be with us. In one sense this is true. Most people are scarred by their families, scarred by their schools, scarred by their society. Mankind is scarred, if you want, but the poor and the members of minority ethnic groups probably bear extra scars. Assuming we have by luck or by strength escaped extra scars, what obligations do we have to the others?

PAUL: I would like first to point out that it is not right to suppose that all the poor live miserable, scarred lives. I don't hold any romantic notions about the poor, but I once was poor myself, and I believe there is a kind of subculture that they live in; they have a kind of confidence in themselves, a kind of completeness, as long as they are not driven to the bare edge of subsistence. My family was not very poor while I was growing up; it had been previously. In any case, I would say we lived a comparatively happy life. I thought you agreed before that those who are living below the subsistence level must be helped to the position where they can live at least in health and without hunger, and without fear of hunger, so that they can actually enjoy some of the goods that accompany daily life in a free country.

JONATHAN: Let me come at this another way. In a sense, some of our greatest pleasures rest on others' miseries. If we go to a theater and see a great play, somebody has to move the scenery, somebody backstage who does not appreciate the play has to lift the curtain, somebody sweeps the stage after the play is over, and so on. The great restaurants are run by many people—busboys, sweepers, etc.—doing tasks that no one would like.

PAUL: I think you're wrong about that. I think that a pride in workmanship exists. I can see that there are dreary and monotonous jobs, but they are not confined to manual labor. Whether a job is monotonous or not usually depends on the person's attitude toward it. I know there are regrettable cases. A man can spend his life on an assembly line doing nothing but putting on the right wheel of a car. That man does have a rotten break. He needs to be educated in such a way that he can make maximum use of all the rest of the time. He must see his work as one of those disagreeable but necessary things that all of us have to do. He does for a longer period what we do when we must take a train or drive a car to get to work. He is subject to certain kinds of necessary conditions somewhat greater than the rest of us, but of the same order. The rest of his time can be enriched in the same way that the rest of our time is enriched.

JONATHAN: I think what you said is outrageous. In the first place, a man is to some degree defined by his job.

PAUL: I would agree with that.

JONATHAN: In the second place, how much time does he have left after work? My memory is that statistical surveys show that people spend at least as many hours working as they did in 1890 because of the necessity for moonlighting. I know that many people in my neighborhood of thirty-five thousand have two jobs. They are either on welfare or working at terrible jobs with long hours.

PAUL: That's not generally the case.

JONATHAN: The figure the poverty program uses is thirty-five million poor. Thirty-five million in a nation of one hundred and ninety is a little over eighteen percent. That's larger than the Jewish and Negro populations of this country combined.

PAUL: I don't deny it, and I've already said that everyone

should be brought up to some reasonable standard of living. But people can also have pride of workmanship, and a rich life apart from their work.

JONATHAN: I think for you to say that a man who makes fifty thousand dollars a year at a boring job is in a position analogous to that of a man who loads trucks eight to ten hours a day in the upper Bronx is ridiculous.

PAUL: Do you think that because a man wears a white collar his work is more interesting?

JONATHAN: I don't think that dealing with the same kinds of stocks and bonds every day is as monotonous as loading the same kinds of groceries on a truck every day. One man does physical labor, is yelled at by other people, and is viewed by society in one way and probably agrees with that view. The other man is viewed by society as doing something meaningful, something with intellectual challenge.

PAUL: I don't think that the man who wears a white collar necessarily has a higher status in the community or a more enjoyable life. I think I would divide the problem into two parts. The first is the work itself. I think almost every man can look at his work as either exciting or debilitating. The second is that a man's life should not be defined in terms of the work he does but in terms of its contribution to a totality; in one portion of that totality he should be able to go beyond what his job requires.

JONATHAN: How much leisure to lead a meaningful life did your father have?

PAUL: My father was working at a time when unions were not as strong as they are today. I'm talking about today and tomorrow in this country.

JONATHAN: I'm talking about today, and I think a large number of people come home too tired to make use of the leisure you talk of.

PAUL: In a way, I agree with this. I think that the ultimate goals of a leisure program can only be attained by the next generation. All we can do for those in this generation who have been cheated is to make it possible for them to enjoy at least a minimum, which they are now being deprived of. The full, rich life they cannot have. Your remarks about the difficulties of creating pride in workmanship and enriching leisure time indicate that the matter is not simple. But a man can, even in a menial job, find some kind of satisfaction and also be able to profit from his leisure.

JONATHAN: How can a man find any sort of meaning in spending eight hours a day pushing a broom on a hot city street sweeping up garbage?

PAUL: Do you mean a broom operated by an automobile?

JONATHAN: No, I mean a broom. In Washington they push a big, thick broom—about one foot wide—down the gutter.

PAUL: I agree with you about the menial character of the job and the low status it has in society. But, as a matter of fact, I have spoken to street cleaners in Washington who found a kind of freedom and ease in their work. To them it wasn't the bitter drudgery you are making it out to be. It isn't a glorious kind of work, but it can be performed with some kind of benefit to the human spirit.

JONATHAN: The old master on a plantation used to say, "You don't know my darkies" and "You don't understand what they're like. I've talked to my darkies and they're happy! Hear them singing in the old cotton fields."

PAUL: I didn't say anything of that nature. I'm just trying to make out that you can't make a black-and-white case the way the old *New Masses* and other communist periodicals in this country used to—as if there were just the downtrodden proletariat, without any kind of hope or future or life or richness, and the other people who were enjoying themselves in a maximum way. I do not think the world is divided into the rich who enjoy themselves enormously and the poor whose lives have no value whatsoever.

JONATHAN: Is this your image of mankind, Western civilized mankind? A sweating Negro pushing a broom in the heart of a ghetto?

PAUL: No, I do not think so. I want to improve that situation.

JONATHAN: Is this man worse off than most men?

PAUL: Yes, I think he is.

JONATHAN: And through no fault of his own?

PAUL: Well, I'm not clear about whether it's altogether not his fault.

JONATHAN: If the man were white and middle class, would he be pushing that broom?

PAUL: He might not be pushing a broom, but he might be living a life that was just as miserable.

JONATHAN: I don't believe that.

PAUL: Yes, he might be condemned by his relatives and might be spending his days in a kind of sodden drunkenness, or engaged in some kind of minor aspect of a business where nobody respected him and where he was functioning very badly. Every night he might come back to an unhappy home. He would be doing less physical labor, but on the whole his life wouldn't be so very different from the other man's. I grant you that if I had to choose between the two jobs, I would prefer not to have the porter's job but instead to have the opportunity that the other man had.

JONATHAN: I've had a number of bad jobs in my life. I had a white-collar job as a lawyer in the Labor Department; I worked with unbelievable hacks, and the job was sheer drudgery. I've also loaded trucks in the Bronx, and believe me, I'd rather work in the Labor Department than load trucks in the Bronx. Further, the rich man has spoiled his own life; the man who pushes a broom has had life spoiled for him.

PAUL: I don't think the problem is that simple. The rich man might have had a terrible upbringing. The poor man, on the other hand, might have had opportunities to go to school, to discipline himself, and to be trained in some particular work, but wished to indulge himself while other people were studying or allowing themselves to be trained. Now, having said that, I agree with you that some men have better opportunities than others. My teacher, Alfred North Whitehead, used to say that he thought the difference between men who made great contributions to civilization and those who did not was a matter of luck, and I agree that there is certainly an element of luck in the career of everybody who has been successful.

JONATHAN: Let me modify my previous statement; I think I sounded too extreme. I think that most people suffer. People can escape slums or shabby neighborhoods as you did. Rich people can have miserable lives. These points are not at issue. What is at issue is the number of strikes against a person or the way in which the whole force of pressures can warp him. You and I do agree that some people could have led more creative lives if they had been luckier. What obligation do we owe them because we have had more luck?

PAUL: I don't think our obligation stems from having had more luck; rather because we had more luck, we have a better opportunity to show our commonality with the rest. And our commonality is precisely the basis of the obligation.

JONATHAN: Perhaps there is a more concrete way to put the question. We have *de facto* segregation in the cities and towns of this country. Some people maintain that we should forcibly integrate schools by busing white students to Negro schools. In general, they argue that we should give Negroes special advantages the whites do not have, to make up for the years of oppression. What do you think of that argument?

PAUL: This raises a very important and difficult issue. I think we ought to separate the problem of *de facto* segregation from the problem of giving special advantages to the underprivileged. I think *de facto* segregation can be remedied by a number of means. We must find a way of persuading the teachers to move about instead of busing the students all over town. I don't think we should take children away from their communities merely for the purpose of having integrated classes. Having integrated classes, unless it is the only opportunity for Negroes to have decent teaching, will not solve the problem of segregation, particularly if the children are then brought back to their segregated neighborhoods. The question of special advantages is more difficult.

JONATHAN: The purpose of the busing is not just to make better teaching available to Negroes but also to enable Negroes to know whites and whites to know Negroes.

PAUL: Yes, but just to know them in class is not really to know them. To know people, one must live with them.

JONATHAN: I agree with you, but it is a step.

PAUL: It is such a minor step that I don't think it's worth the price. I don't think we are attacking the problem of segregation if all we do is have classes where Negroes and whites are together, unless segregated classes inevitably result in poor teaching. But if teaching is adequate in a school where only Negroes attend, I do not think much is solved by bringing whites to that school—if the neighborhood still remains segregated.

JONATHAN: What if the Negroes go to white schools?

PAUL: I still don't think much is solved. The other question is much harder. Should Negroes, instead of being given an equal opportunity, be given a special opportunity so that they can rise to where the others have been, largely because the others have had a long tradition of opportunity?

JONATHAN: More abstractly, should the disadvantaged of a society be given special privileges in society?

PAUL: I have heard it said that most of the higher executive positions in the New York school system are filled by Jews. The Jews claim that they have achieved this dominance through competitive examinations and because of their intellect and industry. Some Negro leaders, however, claim that the Jews have achieved these positions through political pull. Other Negroes say that giving Negroes jobs on the basis of examinations perpetuates the kind of ideology that made it possible for the Jews to succeed. Instead, these jobs should be thought of primarily as political plums and given to Negroes in proportion to their distribution in the population. I think this question is a very hard one to resolve. If administrative jobs in the schools were purely political positions, I would agree with the Negroes who demand their proportionate place. But if these jobs are intimately involved with actual education, I think the Negro must prove himself. The relevant criteria of excellence in a position have to be determined first, and then he who is qualified should be given the post regardless of anything else. If a Negro cannot qualify for one of these positions, we must not give it to him, for if we do we will punish the children who are to be educated under his supervision. And of course what I am saying about the Negroes would apply to any kind of subdivision in our society.

JONATHAN: Let me see if I can summarize this discussion. We both agree that society provides one context for achieving the values of mankind and that this society operates to the disadvantage of some people. As I understand your position, you say the latter fact is really irrelevant when we come to particular choices at particular moments because we must proceed on the basis of merit. It seems to me inequitable not to give disadvantaged people special advantages to compensate for what society has done to them. Nevertheless, I support your position, because I believe that ultimately a person lives as an individual.

PAUL: I am not clear, Jonathan, whether you are agreeing or disagreeing with what I had to say. But let me see if I can give an illustration that might sharpen the issue. It is quite possible that the leading professional teams in baseball, football, and basketball may soon be dominated by Negroes or other minority groups, as prize fighting is so dominated. I do not think that in baseball, for example, we ought to give special privileges to whites or other people who are not able to live up to the high standards set by these Negroes and Puerto Ricans. And just as we want the best baseball players regardless of color, so we want the best teachers and school administrators regardless of color.

JONATHAN: Let us leave that question now and pose another that relates to Negroes. Negroes in this country form, the racists say with some justification, a subculture. Negroes, to some degree, have their ancestral roots in Africa. They have been oppressed. We've been talking about their special rights. Is it possible that they have less rights because they are less a part of Western civilization than we who spring directly from it?

PAUL: Don't forget that America is a country of immigrants and immigrants' children; most of our families have come to the United States in comparatively recent times. Negroes have been here much longer than many whites. There is a certain sense in which one could say that the vast majority of Negroes are more American than the rest of us. The rest of us have ties and affiliations with some other country, whereas the Negro has no such connection. For the most part, he has lost all relationship with Africa; he has no other background than America.

JONATHAN: Aristophanes in Plato's *Symposium* tells a myth of how mankind was once whole and was divided in half by Zeus' thunderbolt. In my opinion, the American Negro was once half of a master-slave relationship. Now that the relationship has been severed, the Negro has to find his own identity, his own culture. He has no upper-class culture the way the fugitives from Europe have.

PAUL: I agree with that.

JONATHAN: Well, let's review what we've covered in this chapter, even if we haven't completed this particular fragment. My doctrine of civilization and our obligation to other men is based on the idea that we collectively embody what greater and lesser men have made the fabric of our daily existence. We have obligations to further our civilization and to help those who make up parts of it. To those who are disadvantaged we have a slightly greater obligation, as long as it is not incompatible with finding our own dignity and as long as it does not prevent us from using qualified people where they are needed. We also recognize the disadvantaged man's essential human identity with us, as we are all men.

PAUL: On the whole I agree with that; I think I have indicated where I don't.

JONATHAN: One brief question. Do we owe any obligation to those who are incapable of understanding the nature of our civilization; for example, retarded children or morons?

PAUL: Our relationship to such people is similar to that which we have to children. We act as their representatives and try to see that they receive as much from life as they can possibly enjoy and profit from.

JONATHAN: My own feeling is that we take care of them because they remind us of humanity and we must be humane to them, but we do not have the obligations to them, except to be decent, that we have to those who are fully able to operate in our society.

5

Man and the Universe

This dialogue focuses on ethics and the nature of the cosmos. The basic question that it confronts is whether or not man makes a difference to the universe, and whether or not there are rational bases for a universal ethics. Among the questions that are raised are the relation that society has to the universe, whether or not there are fundamental realities, and how men are related to what is outside society. Attention is paid to the issue of just what goals men should pursue, whether or not they should seek happiness, and the meaning of "common sense." The discussion ends with observations on the nature of relativity, space, time, and perception.

Paul Weiss emphasizes the distinction between society and the world, at the same time that he relates the one to

the other. Jonathan Weiss relates man and the universe
ethically in terms of common goals and materials. They
agree that there are objective realities, and that there are
proper non-scientific ways of dealing with both space and
time in relation to basic objective realities.

JONATHAN: In the last chapters we discussed first the nature of the
individual; second, his relationship with the family; third,
his role in and ethical obligation to the state; and fourth,
his role in and ethical obligation to society. In this fifth
chapter we'll take up perhaps the greatest of the possible
circles of ethical interest and discuss the nature of the
universe. From the point of view of astronomy, we are but
a speck of microscopic dust in an infinitely vast universe.
So let us start this chapter by my asking you some questions: considering the unlimited space and the apparent
lack of concern of nature for us, what difference does
anything make that we have discussed up to now? Or
more simply, what is the import of the universe for man?
What is the meaning of life?

PAUL: I don't think the fact that we now realize that the universe is so vast really makes a difference. From the
beginning of mankind we've had the problem of building
a civilization in spite of the brute, unreasoning forces of
nature; the whole meaning of life is ultimately tied to the
meaning of a civilized life, or what man can extract of
permanent value through his own interaction with fellow
men and in defiance of nature. And I would say what he
can extract from a civilized life are the fundamental virtues and the fundamental truths which are carried out
and discovered in the sciences and the arts.

JONATHAN: Let me put it another way. When I get up in the morn-
ing and scratch my cheek, it has very little ethical import
because it affects so few things. Whereas, were I to go out
in the street and kill somebody, that would seem to have
large ethical import. Yet if the acts of a single human

being have so little impact on the universe as a whole, perhaps there is no reason to distinguish any ethical act from any other. They may all be equally meaningless in the cosmic sense.

PAUL: If man were nothing more than a unit within the total cosmos, I think I could see some grounds for this conclusion. But the point is that man lives primarily inside a human realm which has been made in spite of the ruthlessness of nature. Man's particular significance lies in the fact that he is a member of a society and ultimately of a civilization which has its own integrity and values and importance; he is not to be flattened out or made to act as though he were nothing more than a subdivision of an unintelligible nature.

JONATHAN: But when you say that society has its own importance, that means that you judge it from some vantage point other than that of society itself.

PAUL: That's correct.

JONATHAN: All right. Then you must find some argument for saying that society has an importance in the scheme of the universe and that man and his acts therefore have some importance. To be able to differentiate one ethical act from another, you must show that man has an impact on the universe other than his impact on human society.

PAUL: If there were nothing more to the universe or the totality of things than society and a space-time cosmos of great magnitude, I think we would have to say what you have just said. But I think there are also other realms which man can come to know by reflection and by faith. Man has an awareness of certain ideals which have a reality apart from brute and unmeaningful nature, and in terms of these ideals we can say that society is not as good as it ought to be. Then there is the relation called faith that some people have to God. There is also the kind of relation that artists sometimes have toward the fundamental drive of existence—intuition. Through reflection, faith, and intuition we come to see basic realities in terms of which man's place in this society and ultimately the meaning of the cosmos can be determined.

JONATHAN: These abstract claims only say that we can come to know something or think we can come to know something of the nature of the universe. It is not the same thing as saying that the nature of the universe is such that society has some value.

PAUL: I don't understand your point very well. These are not abstract claims. There are ultimate realities in terms of which man, society and civilization, and man's hopes and achievements can be judged.

JONATHAN: Perhaps we can separate two issues. One is whether it is possible to judge people by ideals. The other is: regardless of whether or not we can so judge, does mankind have a meaningful impact on the universe? I was asking about the second. You seem to be answering by the abstract claim that the first is true. You seem to be saying that we can understand some aspects of the nature of the universe in terms of which we can judge ourselves, but what you have not answered by this abstract argument is how society or anybody makes any difference to the basic realities so that there is some point, some meaning in our acts.

PAUL: We don't have to make a difference to the world that's outside of society in order to make society be significant. We make use of natural resources in order to build something of a different order. In that different order is where the values lie.

JONATHAN: Values for what?

PAUL: Values which makes life significant.

JONATHAN: For what purpose and in what ways does life affect the universe?

PAUL: It doesn't have to affect the universe.

JONATHAN: Then how can you say it has value?

PAUL: You can have value without affecting the universe.

JONATHAN: But earlier you said life needed to have value which was not derived from society itself.

PAUL: Yes, of course.

JONATHAN: It must then be derived from something else. It must be derived from the nature of the universe.

PAUL: No, no, the values which men obtain are obtained through the use of natural resources. We know of these values not by attending to those natural resources or to what men have made but to other realities beyond both natural resources and man's creations, in terms of which we make our evaluations. They are ideals, absolute standards, eternal beings in the light of which we are able to grade the various activities and achievements of men.

JONATHAN: Let me see if I understand what you're saying. As I understand it, what you are saying is that when we talk about the cosmos we are referring to this abstract notion of it. The universe is a reflection of more fundamental realities. In terms of this realm of fundamental realities we respond by creating something in which we find our meaning. You say somehow by understanding what we've created from fundamental realities we can judge how good a job we did.

PAUL: I think that's more or less what I said, but it's not altogether accurate.

JONATHAN: What is the point of creating society? Why should I care if one society is better in terms of absolute realities than another? What's the point of it?

PAUL: If we had no idea of the nature of the good, of an absolute standard, I do not see how we could answer this question. But I do think we have a knowledge of what is absolutely right and what is absolutely wrong. It is in terms of these basic principles that we make our judgments. We can compare one society with another by studying the degree to which they promote justice and allow men to achieve their maximum happiness, fulfill their promise, and exhibit their potentialities in multiple directions. Any society that encourages these to a greater extent than another is better than that other.

JONATHAN: In other words, your irreducible realities are only people's commonplace homilies and clichés about what they think is good; your realities have no direct connection with any brute forces. If I'm really interested in prosperity and happiness, why should I care about anything else besides my own prosperity and happiness unless it makes some difference somewhere, somehow, to something?

PAUL: The fact that something has been affirmed in the past does not necessarily mean that it is wrong. There is not necessarily anything wrong with clichés, although through overuse they may have lost some sharpness of focus.

JONATHAN: Well, can you focus them sharply again?

PAUL: I will try. We all know the difference between pleasure and pain. Further, we know the difference between happiness and unhappiness, even though we cannot specify the exact content of either one of them.

JONATHAN: As a matter of fact, I'm not sure that's true. We all know about the masochist. We all know that our emotions are transient and that happiness may mean one thing to one person and something else to another. As you pointed out earlier, a parent can tell a child that something is really for his happiness, even though it makes the child unhappy.

PAUL: It's an old observation—it goes back as far as Aristotle—that happiness is not an easily defined term. The fact that we haven't a sharp definition of the objects and operations denoted by happiness does not mean that we haven't a good sense of what the term covers. We know it means that on the whole a man should have on balance more pleasure than pain, that he should have an opportunity to realize the powers of his body and his mind, that he should exercise his will in freedom, that his emotions should come to controlled expression, that he should exhibit himself in creative works, and that he should participate in the betterment of civilization. Men differ in their definitions of happiness, but I would think that any discussion of it would result in something like my present suggestion. I think the difference between one man's judgment of happiness and another's is a difference in range or scope. They do not disagree in the sense that one man says this is a component of happiness and the other man says it positively is not. Rather, they disagree about the number of components sufficient to constitute it.

JONATHAN: Even if a group of people agreed on their abstract characterizations of the nature of happiness, the apparent agreement might simply reflect common ways of expression. Also, they might all agree and all be mistaken. Finally, there is still the problem that an abstract characterization of happiness might cover so many diverse forms of concrete happiness that even a correct agreement about the nature of happiness would not necessarily mean that anybody understood what happiness is for another individual.

PAUL: What does it mean to say that a group of people may be mistaken as to what constitutes happiness?

JONATHAN: It means that the word they use invokes a concept which does not apply to what they are describing. For example, they might say, "Look at those children playing. They are happy," when in fact the children hate each other.

PAUL: Aren't you now saying that happiness must not embrace hatred? If you know that, why can't I know it, and why can't I know other characteristics of happiness?

JONATHAN: No, that wasn't quite what I was saying. In my example, some of the children may have been happy hating; so I couldn't say absolutely that happiness was missing.

PAUL: If the children were happy hating one another, then to say these children are happy is not wrong.

JONATHAN: No, I think it is wrong to simply say all the kids were happy. Some of the kids might be happy, some might be unhappy; all are involved in a complex emotion.

PAUL: Mightn't all the children be happy?

JONATHAN: Yes, but I have no way of knowing. I have no way of knowing for which child hatred is not a happiness and for which child it is a happiness. I do know that in general hatred is not a happy thing, but there are concrete cases where an act of hatred may lead to happiness.

PAUL: If you didn't know what happiness was, I don't think you could say the things you are saying.

JONATHAN: I have my notion of what happiness is, and I empathize with what I think other people think happiness is. It does not mean that there is something which can be categorized as happiness that is common to all men. But let me try to make the point clearer. I can have an abstract doctrine of happiness and can end up with at least two conflicting types of concrete happiness. One man's happiness can be another man's unhappiness.

PAUL: Particular items which make up the content of one man's happy life differ from the items that make up another's. But this does not mean that they wouldn't agree on a basic, common meaning of happiness. For both it requires the realization of their promise and the harmonization of their different powers. For both it means the enjoyment, possession of, and participation in what is excellent. In particular cases they will differ in knowing whether this or that is excellent. It is part of the task of education to show people that what they thought to be excellent is not so and that excellence lies elsewhere. The issue then is not whether two men have altogether different ideas of happiness but whether they have different opinions about what they think is excellent. In some cases they might make a mistake and take that which is less excellent.

JONATHAN: This position creates a thicket of problems for me, some of which I may have indicated. Let me just see if

I can suggest a couple and see how you respond to one which is perhaps essential to them all. I do not know how to adjudicate between two men who both claim that they're after their own happiness, or perhaps even worse, after the happiness of the other. Further, I don't see how you can say that striving for excellence is a component of happiness. We know that people are driven by passions. We know of people for whom happiness is another person's pain. We know that people want things that do not lead to their own happiness. I do not see how we can focus so much on happiness when we have so much trouble understanding what anybody wants, let alone what makes them happy. Finally, why should I care that anybody is happy? Why should I care that I'm happy? What difference does it make in the cosmological scheme of things?

PAUL: The problem of defining what we mean by happiness, like many other basic, vital problems that concern men, has two fundamental answers which are not entirely incompatible. The first is the common-sense answer which is comfortably expressed in clichés. This shows that there is some rough understanding of what happiness is. Your argument makes it clear that there are enough problems involved in these rough statements to make necessary a more subtle understanding of the issue. The task of the philosopher is not to develop an entirely new set of ideas but to clarify what we think we already know. One of the things that we already know is where the good of man lies. The ordinary man quickly becomes confused about the very issues you raised, but it is the function of the philosopher to find the nucleus of meaning within what he is saying, to point out the omissions which characterize his rough understanding, and to clarify the parts he has allowed to remain obscure. Defining happiness, characterizing what is excellent, and finding a way to reconcile men's opposing values are the philosopher's tasks. I was trying to do this before when I characterized happiness as the realization of man's potentialities of mind, body, emotions, and will; his partaking in and contributing to the values that have been achieved in civilization through the arts and sciences; and his exhibiting his creative powers along the lines of his maximum talent. This gives us a generic or broad-based account which each man can fill out according to his own particular experiences and bent. We do not have to justify this account in terms of its effect on the cosmos. It is sufficient that a man by himself, utilizing natural materials and in interaction with his fellow men, has attained an excellence which we can judge in terms of a universal standard of excellence.

JONATHAN: Let me raise three objections to your argument. First, I don't think that the fact that people use common words necessarily indicates that they possess common knowledge. The fact that we use common words may mean only that we have a common understanding of how to communicate in certain situations. Further, what were at one time common understandings have often been discarded as erroneous. The fact that all mankind has agreed, for five thousand years, to use at least in some languages the same sort of word for happiness does not mean that this is not just another fabric of communication. Moreover, if we have to leave it to a philosopher to be our personal guide as to what happiness is, it would be impossible to live intelligently. You claim that not every man need have a conscience, but every man must have a little philosopher tidying along after him with the result that his will is paralyzed. What you say to him is that because you have a common vocabulary you need a philosopher to teach you how to judge. My second objection is that I wanted to know how the universe affected man and whether man affected the universe. You deny that there is any impact, and yet somehow, because men share a common vocabulary, meaning and morality exist. Even if I do share a common vocabulary and a common notion of happiness with other men, why is there an obligation to do anything? Why should I concern myself with this common vocabulary? Finally I come to the objection with which I'm sure you must to some degree agree and that is that happiness is not the only goal. I must have some standard beyond society, beyond common ends, beyond the common vocabulary by which to adjudicate the various conflicting or, if you want, complementary ends of society. To explain the ethical import of the universe or man's role by saying philosophers must clarify commonly understood words about goals raises more questions than it answers.

PAUL: Let me start with the third point. In one sense of course you are right. Man seeks a higher good than happiness. Happiness is a word we use to characterize man when he has achieved these highest goods. It is a term which is indefinite precisely because the definite content is given by higher goods, such as the achievements of civilization. But let me return now to your first point, which is perhaps more important. I do not think it correct to say that the common-sense outlook is wholly mistaken.

JONATHAN: That's not my claim. I think it is wrong to talk about common sense as if all people are born with a similar vision, which philosophers can clarify. Rather, people develop a common vocabulary as they grow up. This common vocabulary quite often expresses what seem to be common ideas and we sometimes call this common sense.

PAUL: In all societies throughout history, there has existed a common awareness of the importance of birth, death, adolescence, and the transition to manhood. Man has also recognized the need for health and the right of the individual to be distinct from others. The awareness of the importance of these values and of life stages is expressed in holidays, celebrations, and rituals. No one needs a philosopher to tell him the importance of these common events. A philosopher is necessary to clarify their meaning, to deal with them systematically and critically, and to relate them to other aspects of life. We should try to justify our ethical judgments by references to a fundamental domain of ultimate, ideal realities, and final standards. This of course is a philosophical observation, not a common-sense one. It is the observation of one trying to find a base in terms of which common-sense judgments can be evaluated.

JONATHAN: I think this is an excellent statement as far as it goes. I agree that men exhibit common responses and hold common ideals and that these reflect something beyond the individual and perhaps beyond society. But that still does not get us to common sense. The fact that people have common responses to common ideals is not a basis for saying that people who have a common vocabulary express in a rough way fundamental values in terms of which I can understand the import of the universe for all of us. Nor does the fact that people act in this way therefore mean that people *should* act in this way.

PAUL: I agree. But I think that any point of view which in the end does not accept and justify a large portion of what men, over the generations, have taken to be good, runs the risk of being impractical and of talking in terms of what you call mere abstractions. The function of all our sciences and our philosophy is to clarify what we in some sense already know, not to discover something which we do not know at all, and certainly not to discover something which rejects all that we know as common-sense men. If they did reject everything we know as common-sense men, they would in the end destroy the very evidence on which science and philosophy themselves depend.

JONATHAN: I think your defense of common sense is mistaken because all common sense reflects is the operation on the world of a particular perspective. It may incidentally reflect truth because a particular perspective may be grounded in straightforward perception and traditional doctrines of learning.

PAUL: But I agree with that. I agree that ordinary common sense is shot through with superstition—

JONATHAN: But that's not what I am objecting to. I am saying that men don't start with common sense. Any notion a man holds will somehow be related to notions other people held in the past and to the common perceptual features of mankind. I'm not convinced yet that the common perceptual features and common perceptual understandings of mankind are found by referring to common sense.

PAUL: Maybe we can narrow our disagreement a little by making a distinction. The world of common-sense man is a rather restricted one. His purview usually goes no further than his own limited experiences and the outlook of his own particular society. So far as this is true of a given man, he certainly hasn't grasped the fundamental realities. Yet contained within this particular specialized outlook is a more basic one which I would call a kind of fundamental common sense. It is that to which I was referring. That fundamental common sense is a characteristic not only of a man in a given society or at a given time but of all men at all times. And I would say it exists because man is not only a being in society but a cosmological being, or better, an ontological being. He is related to whatever realities there are, not just to whatever may exist in space and time. He is related to ultimate ideals, to God, to the nature of what I call Actuality, the Being within which all particular beings are.

JONATHAN: To avoid confusion, why don't you state briefly what you mean by God.

PAUL: The term "God," as you know, has had many different meanings over the course of time, in both the East and the West. But I think we come close to a common usage if we say that God is an ultimate being, permanent and spiritual, to whom man must adjust himself in some way in order to become as fulfilled a being as possible. God is the point toward which man must direct himself if he is to achieve a maximization of all his values and in harmony.

JONATHAN: Since your doctrine of fundamental common sense did not succeed in narrowing our disagreement, perhaps it would help if I stated my position on the relation of man to the universe. First, I believe that everything has many characteristics and levels of characteristics. A table can be looked at as a spatial object, as a collection of molecules, as an art object, as the cause of an emotion, and so on. Every single thing I perceive therefore has various levels of meaning and being which I can understand. Second, it seems to me that the universe is in flux. I also believe, although I won't try to justify my belief here, that it's moving from somewhere to somewhere. I would argue for a type of teleology, resting on ultimate purpose. Mankind enters the scene in a manner suggested by Pascal's statement that man is but a frail reed whose thought encompasses the universe. Man has the ability to understand all these various levels, and most important, the creative ability to do something lasting. He can abstract from all the various modes of experience and build something which reflects all these basic levels. Therefore I would say mankind has an impact on the universe because man is able to abstract from reality various important levels and somehow embody these levels in works of art. In this way he fulfills what is cosmologically incomplete, what needs mankind to fulfill it. Therefore, mankind is important in relation to the universe, because he is creative. He understands by abstracting and responding. He gets involved by creating. The end of mankind is to be creative, to increase the amount of beauty and art in this world.

PAUL: I like much of what you have said, although I don't see any warrant for supposing that the universe starts from some particular point and moves in a definite direction toward some other presumably higher point, or that man is contributing to this movement. I think it more correct to say that the universe itself is brute, that it has no direction or purpose. Direction and purpose derive from men who reflect upon what they have been doing and what they want to attain. Man's task is not to increase the beauty of nature: the beauty he makes is of a different order entirely. The beauty of a statue or a painting, though it can be characterized in the same way as natural beauty, is not in itself natural beauty. One does not add to the totality of the beauties of nature by producing works of art.

JONATHAN: It seems to me that you have already conceded enough in your answer to enable us to come to an agreement. When you say artistic creation is altogether of a different order from natural beauty, you admit that man has created something that did not exist before. Only man could put elements of the universe together in this new combination. A genuine art of creation not only adds something new but, as you said earlier, involves a response to something in the world. The created comes from real elements and has a real existence. What this means is that in some sense the world is a more complete place because of man's creations. Or, putting it the other way around, you might say that the fact that man can create means that there is a need for his creations. I would argue that the recognition that mankind responds to the world, the recognition that there is a genuine art of creation, is sufficient to indicate that we are completing what is incomplete in the world and therefore doing something more proper and more ethical.

PAUL: Though man is part of the total scheme of things, he is not functioning fully as a man until, with other men, he becomes part of a human realm. This human realm has its own values, its own rhythm, its own history. The

169

contributions man makes are to that human realm, and it is in this human realm that his basic values and achievements are to be found. His contributions then are not to the cosmos as a whole but just to that delimited portion of it within which he lives. There his fundamental insight into the nature of things is shaped into a common-sense outlook.

JONATHAN: Our positions don't seem to me incompatible, although I think mine is more inclusive. I think one of the things mankind contributes to the cosmos is civilization. I would say that everything I do is done within the context of humanity and also within the context of the cosmos. Humanity and civilization are good for the cosmos. If I am creative, my particular act is good for mankind and for the cosmos, and therefore I say the end of civilization is to make it possible for men to be as creative as possible. Such a doctrine requires the recognition of all people's individual worth and the encouragement of people pursuing beauty, coupled with the recognition that one must keep open as many opportunities as possible in which to act and in which to be creative.

PAUL: I think you are suggesting a view similar to one I once held—that man is essentially a being who belongs to the totality of things, and that he acts with respect to that totality.

JONATHAN: Yes, that is my view, but I also believe that he acts within a limited range.

PAUL: In that case, your position is close to mine. The issue now is, what is the nature of this larger world? I think we must distinguish the cosmos, or existence, which is spatial, temporal, and dynamic and generally the subject of theoretical science, from God. The two have sometimes been identified. But they are distinct; God is not spatial or temporal in the sense in which the world or realm of existence is, though I think we can say with Spinoza that God has a kind of extensionality.

JONATHAN: What do you mean by space?

PAUL: Space is extended and contemporaneous. Parts of space are spatial, said Kant; I think that's correct. Space is made up of relations of next to nextness. Using the term "dimension" the way mathematicians use it, to mean that which is expressed by independent variables, space can be said to have an indefinite number of dimensions.

JONATHAN: Let me ask some naïve questions. We quite often use the word "space" to mean nothingness. If there is emptiness between Mars and the earth, how can we be distant from one another?

PAUL: Space is extended; there is a distance between its terms. But when we equate space with nothingness, what we really mean is that the distance has no content within it, that we have nothing but sheer relation. However, many cosmologists would say that space is never wholly empty, that it is not a vacuum but is thinly populated.

JONATHAN: What is it that is between the two terms and is so thinly populated?

PAUL: I would say what is between them is an extended, symmetrical distance.

JONATHAN: Do objects constitute space?

PAUL: No. Space is not a thing. Space is a dimension, an aspect of existence, the way time is, and the way a law of nature is. It is not an object like a table or a chair but a structure or an aspect of these, extending beyond any one of them and embracing all of them.

JONATHAN: Which of the following three definitions of space would you agree with: Kant's definition of space as a perceptual presupposition of all objects; a definition of space as being presupposed by objects; or a definition of space as created by objects so that the two somehow are manifestations of something beneath them and are therefore interrelated? I think I myself am closest to the third. Are you?

PAUL: No, I think I hold a fourth position. There is a space that is not constituted by any particular objects. Even if there were no things, space would still exist as sheer extensionality. On the other hand, the objects which are in the world are themselves extended. The chair itself is this particular limited space vivified. It is the very space at the place which it occupies. So we can think of an object as a kind of intensified form of space. Or we can think of space itself as a kind of attenuated form of the space in objects. Objects move about in the space and are constituted in other ways; some of them—for example, men—have minds or selves which are not necessarily spatially defined. Moreover, they also exist in another dimension, time. So you cannot identify objects with space itself. Nor would I say that everything must be spatial and temporal; God and ideals are not.

JONATHAN: Your position assumes that these ideals are not artifactual but somehow real. One difficulty with this assumption is that we're saying either that space is an element with no objects or that space defines all objects. If we say it is an element, we somehow vitiate what it is.

PAUL: That's right.

JONATHAN: On the other hand, to say that space defines objects gives it a power that it does not appear to have in its purest form.

PAUL: I would like to make a distinction between three kinds of entities. One: particular objects such as tables, chairs, human beings, books, dogs, houses, wind. Two: dimensions or aspects of whatever exists, such as space, time, causation, laws of nature. Three: beings or ultimate realities such as existence, God, and the realm of possibility. Space is a dimension of our ultimate reality, and exists regardless of whether there are particular objects. But particular objects always exist within space, that is, within a dimension of this ultimate reality I call existence.

JONATHAN: Why is it that space by itself has no power, and yet when it is in an object it helps constitute it?

PAUL: An object itself could be said to be geometrizing total space, vivifying it, and giving it an intensified form in a particular location. Space as a whole has a minimal being and a minimal geometry. This geometry and this being are intensified and distorted, if you like, by the objects said to be in space.

JONATHAN: But let us pose an apparent opposition. Einstein, as most people understand him, popularized the idea that there is no such thing as space in itself, that space is a function of something else. Einstein never talks about space in the way that we've been talking about it.

PAUL: I was not talking as a physicist when I characterized the nature of space. I was talking about the nature of the real world. Physics is engaged in trying to find explanations for what can be observed to function in law-abiding ways. Einstein found a basic explanation which could be applied to a multiplicity of laws, particularly to the transmission of light over vast space. In his account, space and time functioned purely as structures. They are not necessarily extended, and they certainly do not relate objects such as tables and chairs to one another. They are abstract formulations of a rationalistic sort serving to provide an explanation of law-abiding activities.

JONATHAN: Do you think time is more basic than space, that space is an extension of time?

PAUL: No.

JONATHAN: What then is time?

PAUL: When Augustine was first asked this question, he said, "I know what time is until somebody asks me and then I don't know." It is one of the most difficult notions in the history of thought. It has been the object of much philosophical study, and usually results in the formulation of odd paradoxes. The tendency of all talk about time, as Bergson said, is to spatialize it, to rigidify it. I think the wisest way to begin a discussion of time is to recognize what all of us in some sense do know—but which very few theories acknowledge—that there are many different kinds of time. There is a time of physical occurrences; there is a time of history; there is a time of religious history; there is a time of biological growth; a time of evolution; a time of music; a time of the theater; a time of emotional involvements; and so on. All of these have in common the fact that they are ordered in a serial way; that there is an earlier and a later; a past, a present, and a future. I think we can bring these multiple times into a manageable set by distinguishing those cases in which time is monotonous and non-accumulative from those cases in which it fluctuates and is accumulative. In physics we have a monotonous, repetitive time. Each moment is as large as the preceding one; nothing that lives through such time learns anything from the fact that it had been in existence before. In biological time, however, we add to our present what we experienced in the past; what we do at one moment is affected by what was done before. Time has different rhythms by virtue of this accumulation. It extends out in some moments, it contracts in others. It rushes forward, it slows down; it has peaks and valleys. These characteristics depend on the nature of its content. I do not think we can really understand time apart from its content. But to the degree that we can, I suppose it must be something close to the physicists' idea of it—repetitive, monotonous, and non-accumulative.

JONATHAN: Could we not say that when we use the word "time" we recognize the fact that the universe is in a process of change, that somehow the relationship of things produces an alteration which we characterize as time; hence it has different meanings?

PAUL: Your view certainly has the sanction of one of the greatest of all philosophers, Aristotle. He defined time as the number of change and motion. But I think that there could be time without change and motion. Unlike

Aristotle, I would say it makes sense to say that nothing happened for a long time.

JONATHAN: As a lawyer I will rest with authority; let's end the chapter at this point.

6

Law

The final discussion of the book focuses on law. Common law, positive law, and natural law are discussed and distinguished. The discussion then deals with the problems of judicial decision and the principles which underlie it. Crimes and indebtedness are examined in the light of the principles set down. The application of law and the relation of law and politics are treated. The discussion closes with a consideration of the justification of civil disobedience—one of the main threads running throughout the dialogues.

Paul Weiss maintains that "justice" should be a controlling factor in the determination of the status of law and the decisions of judges. Jonathan Weiss insists that law is a special domain, and that its demands are not subject to personal, particular principles of morality. They agree that there is a natural law, and that an international law is as yet nonexistent.

PAUL: Jonathan, I would like now to ask you some questions, particularly about the law. Do you have a definition of the law that would apply to all forms of it?

JONATHAN: Not really. I think the best way to approach the problem of defining law is similar to Aristotle's approach to definition in his *Metaphysics*. The word "law" has a lot of different meanings, but in back of all these meanings is a common concept. Yet I don't think we can define that concept by itself or derive it from definitions of particular cases. We have to describe law both in an ideal sense and in a particular sense that reflects its operations. Law in the ideal sense exists, I think, when a common governing body promulgates a written rule that people can and do apply clearly—that is, everybody understands what it means not to obey it. But all these factors may not be present. For one thing, people may not understand what the law means. To most people it may read one way; to judges, another. It can be a statute on the books, not followed, not obeyed, not evoked, what we call a dead-letter law. Or it can be a law which people believe is there, or followed by habit, but is not really written down. It can be without a clear, simple meaning. It can be a law which is overturned because the judges or the governing authorities don't think it is a law. It can have all these different, more limited meanings. So I would say briefly that a law is something which has one of these characteristics: it is applied by judges, promulgated by the state, obeyed by the people, or exists in writing. The idea in a sense includes all these.

PAUL: Could we not make a more basic distinction between

common law and positive law; that is, law which is carried out according to a traditional policy and laws which are actually forged by the legislature and written out?

JONATHAN: No. Common law grew up in England as a series of principles which evolved from settling disputes. Judges went from town to town settling disputes. When they found common disputes, they tried to evoke common rules, to give some sort of consistency and coherence to their governing. I think practically every jurist would call the doctrine they created positive law. The only difference between it and the law promulgated by legislative authority is that it was generated by judges settling disputes. It did not grow out of a common heritage; rather, it created a common heritage.

PAUL: Are you denying that there is any significant difference between common and positive law?

JONATHAN: Yes.

PAUL: Would you say that there is such a thing as natural law?

JONATHAN: Yes, I would. I would say that all laws in some sense reflect common principles. Some people argue that the minimum requirement of a legal system is coherence, but I don't think that is so. Laws function to give people rules to live by. I think the ultimate aim of law in general is to provide a means of settling disputes, a means of establishing order and common expectations of conduct, and a device for achieving the values of civilization by defining how men ideally should act.

PAUL: I don't think that answers my question about natural law.

JONATHAN: What I'm saying is that law as it now exists reflects natural law in two ways. First, it defines how men ideally should act. In this sense it embodies natural law in concrete form. And second, in providing a system for men to live together and settle disputes, it embodies the fact that we wish to preserve certain values. The values in question are those we usually mean when we talk of natural law. I think we also have to take into account natural rights and natural principles. Natural rights are those rights presupposed or defined by the nature of mankind. Any system of law has to recognize certain basic rights, and therefore we can talk of a common law that lies beneath all laws. In other words, there is a natural law based on mankind that provides for all legal systems a doctrine of natural rights.

PAUL: When a judge makes a decision, particularly a Supreme Court justice, does he look to natural law for guidance or as a check?

JONATHAN: Do you mean in actual practice or ideally?

PAUL: Ideally.

JONATHAN: One of the judge's intellectual tasks is to understand the meaning of the words, categories, and concepts with which he is dealing. He has to apply a particular law to a particular problem. Sometimes to understand the meaning of that law or to resolve ambiguities, he may have to have recourse, for example, to the intention of the legislature. By intention I don't mean the particular motivation of the individual legislators. Rather, he may have to have recourse to an abstract idea of natural law as revealed in legislative intent. I don't think this happens often, though.

PAUL: But people have disagreed over the years on whether there is natural law, and if there is, what it embraces. I do not see how a judge, following your suggestions, would know where to turn to make sure that he was referring to natural law and not to his own prejudices about what the legislature sought to do.

JONATHAN: Very good. I myself hold to a doctrine of traditional absolutes and of applying the law as most obviously written just because I think there's a danger that when we say we've adopted a natural law what we're doing is allowing the judge to follow his own bent as to what he thinks is right and just. I think Justice Black, over the twenty-five years or so he has been on the Supreme Court, has pointed out time and time again that when people evoke natural law and the dignity of mankind they allow themselves to infringe the absolutes of the Constitution; they are not enhancing freedom and dignity as they claim. More directly, there are no good written sources that a judge can use for practical guidance on matters of natural law. What the judge can do is to argue that words and concepts like due process, property, witness, freedom, controversy, and federalism are abstract nouns that have acquired varying concrete contents over the years so that when we use these words we have to have recourse to some sort of abstract category beyond them. Thus, when the judge is involved in an ambiguous situation, he may have to invoke these abstract ideas.

PAUL: I don't see how he is to know how to proceed. Having found that something is ambiguous in the context of positive law, how does he move to some basic categorical meaning which will help clarify and even test the ordinary usages?

JONATHAN: I think he's supposed to resolve a particular dispute and perhaps express broad guidelines for future law-conforming conduct. To do that, he has to look for the basic principles that are embodied in decisions, rather than mechanically balancing previous decisions or looking to what the legislature has said. He has to refer to a rationale behind the law, and if that is not sufficient, he must infer from the whole judicial system the rationale behind that. And if that is not sufficient, I think he will practically always refer to the rationale behind all laws. He must in fact engage in the process of abstraction and inference, but he must do this in a very clear way, so that it is a process of logical reasoning and reduction rather than a sudden invocation of abstract principles.

PAUL: In other words, he takes account of the nature of man?

180

JONATHAN: I think eventually he might be forced to refer to the nature of man.

PAUL: Now it is a fact, is it not, that philosophers disagree with one another as to what the nature of man is, and all of them together disagree with biologists, and the two groups together disagree with sociologists, and all of them together disagree with politicians. What is the poor judge to do when he wants to find out the nature of man so that he can have a sensible base for his judicial judgments?

JONATHAN: I tried to answer this question earlier. When I say he infers from the systems of law and the decisions and legislative pronouncements that embody the legal concept of man, he infers from these concrete contexts as much as he needs to arrive at a more basic concept of man, which he then brings back into his legal system.

PAUL: I wonder if I could put my question a little more abstractly in order to focus on it better. Let's distinguish two words, the "immanent" and the "transcendent." The immanent is that which I have immediately; the transcendent is that which is beyond the immediate. It seems to me there are two kinds of transcendent. One is a transcendent relative to the immediate, that which is always beyond it. For example, the front of this chair is immanent but the back of the chair is transcendent relative to that immanence. The other meaning of transcendent refers to something which is detached from that which I have immediately. For example, in Plato's philosophy the chair has a form which exists in eternity regardless of whether or not there were any chairs. I make these distinctions because it's not clear to me whether, when you're speaking about natural law, you're talking about a relative transcendent (which is what it seems to me you were talking about recently) or whether you are referring to an absolute transcendent (which is what I thought you were talking about at the beginning).

JONATHAN: Very good. There are two separate questions. The first is whether there is such a thing as natural law, and the second is the way in which a judge can utilize the concepts of natural law. Answering the first question, I would maintain that there is a natural law which exists beyond and independent of particular legal systems.

PAUL: Therefore an absolute transcendent?

JONATHAN: An absolute transcendent. As to the second, I would say that a judge need not necessarily have recourse to this absolute transcendent, because I think the natural law is reflected and embodied in the particular legal systems. A judge has to reach a decision by applying inferences from cases to particular problems. He need not have recourse to the embodied abstraction but need only refer to whatever part of it is embodied in his system.

PAUL: I'm bothered by that somewhat. It seems to say that a Nazi judge could do nothing more than get a relative transcendent to the Nazi legal system and therefore would not really be able to make the kind of judgment that would have been made by reference to absolute transcendent natural law.

JONATHAN: There were values embodied in the Nazi legal system which we share, as you pointed out in an earlier chapter; these values reflect natural law.

PAUL: Can you illustrate some of those common values?

JONATHAN: Due process is an example. The job of a trial is to arrive at the truth, not to achieve a predetermined result. The Nazi judges imprisoned people and condemned them to death because they were told to. They did not apply principles of law in their trials.

PAUL: Wouldn't the kind of natural law that would be abstracted by such a judge be quite different from the one that our judges might abstract?

JONATHAN: I think you may be driving at a problem we will have to discuss later. That is, when does a law become not a law? But as far as this example goes, no, the legal system purported to be a legal system.

PAUL: Could you state what you think the common objective of all legal systems is?

JONATHAN: I thought I stated that earlier. The objective is three-fold: to allow people to settle disputes; to help establish a society in which men may find themselves; and to lay down an ideal to which men may respond. A cliché you often hear is that the law cannot legislate morality, but that is precisely what the vast majority of enactments do.

PAUL: To a philosopher, what you just said is astonishing because of a strange omission. I was straining to hear you say that justice is the objective of the law. But instead you said the objective is to settle disputes and to keep public order. Would you care to say a word about justice, and why you didn't mention it?

JONATHAN: Yes. I think justice was implicit in what I said, but let me make it explicit now. To settle disputes fairly, establish an ideal for men, and set up a society in which people can achieve goals—this is all related to justice. I think you were thinking only of the first category, that is, of the just achievement of disputes, settlement with justice, the idea that there is a right or just way to resolve all disputes. But I think it may be true that there is no one right or just way to solve a particular dispute, and I don't think justice is a criterion by which we can judge all decisions. We have a system for solving disputes because in order to live together, people must have common expectations.

PAUL: I see that in part. Before I deal with it, I want to say that I am not yet clear about the relationship between relative and absolute transcendent natural law. If there is a connection between them, why shouldn't a judge refer to the absolute in order to clarify those factors which cause him to diverge from other judges?

JONATHAN: If I understand you properly, he should not for precisely the reasons you suggested. If the man says he knows the absolute, then he is really not applying law but at best, his own doctrines of understanding the absolute

and at worst, mere prejudice. Whereas if the man uses
the law to arrive at his decision, we have a way of check-
ing him.

PAUL: Well, what is the relationship of the second result to
the first result?

JONATHAN: I think that judges do not achieve natural law by abstraction, though philosophers may arrive at their understanding of it that way. Rather, judges usually derive natural law from particular legal systems. Insofar as legal
systems are generated by men striving for an ideal, they
reflect a natural law. That is why a judge can refer in
each individual legal system to doctrines which somehow
embody natural law, and therefore have a type of natural-
law reference in his decisions.

PAUL: Do you really think that you can find in the law of
South Africa today, particularly as it applies to the Negroes, and in Nazi law at the time when the Nazis were in
power, principles which illustrate an absolute transcendent natural law, to which the judges do not themselves
attend but which is exemplified within their legal system?

JONATHAN: I would say that there was a rule of law in Nazi Germany. They did have trials. However, in those cases in
which the judge only pretended to have a trial, he was
simply acting outside the law. Here we are similarly out-
raged when we read that a judge receives a letter from a
congressman about somebody who is pleading a case
before him, and that person wins. We say we had the pre-
tense of the law but not the actuality of it.

PAUL: But Hitler could have said such and such is the law.
Don't we then have a positive law to which a judge must
pay attention?

JONATHAN: There are two steps to be made. Suppose a judge is
faced with a law that says all Jews must be killed. In one
sense it is a law. The judge must now decide what his
duty is toward that law; he must also decide what his duty

is in applying that law. Now I think there is a time when we must cease being judges. We have further obligations that must be met, and therefore the job of the judge is either to quit or to make his own law.

PAUL: What would tell him it is intolerable?

JONATHAN: I think he must decide not as a judge but as a man understanding the nature of the world. More, he must act as a philosopher and as a moral being.

PAUL: You don't think he decides on the basis of the absolute natural law?

JONATHAN: I think the absolute natural law might tell him this, but not in his role as a judge.

PAUL: Now I think we're close to something. What you're saying, if I understand you, is that a judge as a human being has some kind of insight into the absolute natural law, but when he functions within a legal system he applies only the relative guise of the natural law, which he can obtain from some kind of inference from his legal system. When there is a conflict between the two, is it the absolute natural law which has precedence?

JONATHAN: No, not entirely. "Absolute natural law" does not necessarily have precedence. It depends on an evaluation of importance. In other words, I think a judge must come to some decisions which he believes are unjust, which perhaps even violate what appears to be natural law. Let me give you a clear instance of this. Suppose I am a lower court judge and a constitutional issue comes up. I think the Supreme Court is wrong in terms of the Constitution and wrong in terms of how the Constitution embodies natural law. Nonetheless, I believe I'm constrained to follow that precedent as a judge. Only in certain extreme cases where applying the law blindly would be so destructive to mankind that it destroyed law itself would I either quit or violate the law. I would say, only where I violate natural law and harm mankind so thoroughly as to destroy the point of the legal system do I have a right to overrule my relative judgments by the absolute.

PAUL: Would you remark as to where you think that point would be? I would like to touch upon the question of morality and law.

JONATHAN: Before we get to that, let me make my second point, which is that the judge has to play along even when it is unjust, even when, perhaps, it destroys the fabric. That is, even suppose the law says all Jews must be killed. A person still has the right to a trial determining whether or not he is a Jew. There is not only the point that we refer to principles when a judge becomes a man and has a duty in his judging, but also in the judging there is a *process* to be gone through. Now I would say the purpose of judges is to function in civilization. When I in fact make a judgment that would destroy members of mankind in large segments or destroy the fruits of civilization, then I say I destroy the purpose of the whole legal system and I therefore have a right to quit the legal system.

PAUL: I think I sense your intention, and with that I agree. But what you say explicitly bothers me. There have been historical periods when those in power have decided that art was decadent and, for the protection of their people, have decided it should no longer be practiced. Whether this is a wise measure is one question. But to say that a judge should leave the bench because this denial of art goes counter to his understanding of the fundamental obligations of a man seems rather extreme. Even today in the United States, where there are all kinds of art that the legislature might ban, I doubt whether any judge would think it was incumbent upon him to resign rather than to carry out the legislature's decrees.

JONATHAN: I don't think art could be banned in this country because of the First Amendment, but let's in any case make the problem more clear-cut. Would it bother you if a judge quit the bench because a law was passed saying that every second baby must be killed?

PAUL: Yes, because I myself would hold a much stronger doctrine of natural law and make the judge responsible to it. I would say that in every case where there is a conflict, positive law must yield to the fundamental natural law. Let's see if we can bring this issue to bear on a more realistic situation related to morality and law. You said before, if I remember correctly, that most of the law was essentially moralistic.

JONATHAN: No, I didn't say that. I said that we legislate morality and try to evoke ideals that enable men to live together, but the application of law does not proceed by utilizing the judge's moral values. You seem to say a judge should engage in civil disobedience of not following his oath to follow the law when he finds a law repugnant to "natural" law. Such an act is as a man, not a judge. And although perhaps more politically effective, he violates his word and role. He should resign rather than resist.

PAUL: Let's make a distinction between morals and ethics. Morals refers to the conventional mores, the way people are accustomed to behave in public as decent and harmonious members of a single society; ethics refers to absolute principles that apply to all mankind even though they may never be actually realized. We can say that law is essentially an instrument of morality. It doesn't follow, though, that the law will necessarily be in consonance with the demands of ethics.

JONATHAN: I think we can have bad laws; is that what you are saying?

PAUL: A bad law is one which does not conform to ethical principles.

JONATHAN: It is also one that does not serve the good goals of society.

PAUL: Could a law be consonant with ethical principles and violate people's sense of what is right and wrong?

JONATHAN: A law could. A judge may not.

PAUL: Well, now, if this is the case, it raises the question you mentioned before: when is a law not a law?

JONATHAN: I think a law is clearly not a law when it cannot be applied because it is confusing or contradictory to itself, or, as I suggested earlier, to what the legal system as a whole is designed to serve.

PAUL: That is exactly what I wanted to get at. What do you say about a law which conforms to ethical principles but which goes so counter to the practices, ideals, attitudes, and understanding of the people that it is unenforceable?

JONATHAN: There is no such thing as an unenforceable law that I can think of. Give me an example. Suppose we suddenly decreed that all people must drive on the left-hand side of the road. Well, it would be a difficult law to apply, but we could enforce it.

PAUL: Suppose in a country such as Pakistan a dictator prescribed that everybody must eat pork. It would go so counter to the practices and outlook of the people that I think they would revolt. Would that be a law?

JONATHAN: It would be a law.

PAUL: But it would go counter to the moral practices of the people. Suppose the dictator based his law on hygienic or ethical principles. Would the situation then simply be an example of what you brought up in an earlier chapter, that all people must do some things that are undesirable?

JONATHAN: Yes. After all, the Mormons were confronted with a law outlawing polygamy. Prohibition was imposed by law.

PAUL: Then I don't understand when a law is not a law.

JONATHAN: A law is not a law when it cannot be applied. Suppose I passed a law saying all men must fly.

PAUL: That's unenforceable. I see there is a subtle difference here. I said a law was not a law when it was unenforceable, but you said no, all laws are enforceable. Now I gather that what you are calling inapplicable laws are what I call unenforceable laws. We cannot enforce a law which says that man should walk and swim at the same time.

JONATHAN: Well, no, because by its nature it is impossible. A self-contradictory law is unenforceable as a consequence of being inapplicable, whereas an ethically inapplicable law may be only difficult to enforce.

PAUL: I grant you that, but aren't there laws that are unenforceable precisely because they go counter to the entire practice of mankind, and not because they are self-contradictory?

JONATHAN: I think it would be foolish to say that Prohibition wasn't a law just because so many people resisted it. To the degree to which it was honored in the breach, it was not law in the perfect sense. Some laws are laws only in an extremely attenuated sense.

PAUL: What about international law? Is there such a thing as international law?

JONATHAN: I don't think so, although my position is an extremely unpopular one. The official argument for international law is that there are common references, arbiters, and principles based on sanctions that can be imposed because of the pressure of nations. There are common codes; there are agreements; there are treaties. Over the years, traditions of respect for nations and their internal decrees have produced both public and private international law. My own feeling is that there is no central body which promulgates authoritatively. Based on no common references, not referring to individuals under a common collectivity, international law is a misnomer for adaptable patterns of international dealings. International law is as strong as the agreement between the nations who believe in it, and as meaningful as individual nations want to make it by following a pattern of action.

PAUL: That only points up the fact that our previous definition of law was incomplete. There cannot be a law without enforcement. Something stated by a legislature is not yet a law. A law must be backed by power which will make it applicable to concrete situations.

JONATHAN: I don't think that's correct. The reason I didn't mention power before is that I think law can exist without having explicit force behind it. For example, a law can exist that all people want to have and want to follow. It is a principle of law that a judge must give reasons for his decision. There is hardly a way to enforce this principle, and in fact quite a few judges unfortunately don't follow it. Quite a few judges act arbitrarily. There is really no force or sanction to be applied against the judge who does not give reasons for his decisions. Nevertheless, we can say that it is the law that a judge must give reasons. It is a law because we expect judges to do so and because judges say they are going to do so. But there is no sanction that can be applied to a judge who does not in effect give reasons.

PAUL: You mean there is a law which says that the judge must give reasons?

JONATHAN: Not on the books. There is a body of doctrine which says judgment shall be based on reason.

PAUL: I don't see that that's a law. It may be customary for a judge to give reasons, but since there is no sanction if he doesn't, I would say it conforms to what you said about international law—that there is no international law precisely because there are no sanctions.

JONATHAN: If I am involved in a case in which a judge gives a decision with no reason, I can make an appeal on the grounds that the law says a judge must give a reason, and an appeal court will reverse the judge if he has not given a reason. Although there is no sanction, the judge has not acted properly and can be reversed.

PAUL: But I thought you said there is no such law. So, to what would you appeal?

JONATHAN: I would quote a case which says a judge must give a reason.

PAUL: You're referring to precedent?

JONATHAN: Right.

PAUL: But precedent is only a kind of custom. Custom and law are not identical, are they?

JONATHAN: As I pointed out earlier, the common law becomes positive law and the roots of common law *are* in custom. There is no question that precedents make law in the American and the English systems. There is no statute which says a man may not break into another man's house after dark with intent to commit a felony there. But that's the common law of burglary, and a man can be convicted on the common-law precedents that define that crime.

PAUL: But doesn't it say something in the Constitution about the rights of property?

JONATHAN: Yes, but the Constitution does not define crimes. The common-law crime of burglary was defined by a series of cases which said that when someone is caught entering a man's dwelling after dark with the intention of committing a felony, he is liable for burglary. In fact, what legislatures have done now to expand that common-law crime is to pass statutes against what they call house-breaking, because they want to be able to arrest people for felonious entry during the day.

PAUL: I'm getting confused. You say the Constitution has nothing to do with criminal law?

JONATHAN: It does not define crimes.

PAUL: How about holding a man in double jeopardy? Isn't that a criminal situation?

JONATHAN: Treason is the only crime defined in the Constitution. The Constitution does establish substantive rights in criminal process and safeguards for criminal procedure, but safeguards and rights don't define crimes. The most you can say is that the Constitution gives us the ability to pass laws concerning crime. And in fact what I was saying earlier was that there are common-law crimes which have never been written down in the books; they are still crimes.

PAUL: Then are customary procedures that have been established in the course of the conduct of the law themselves laws?

JONATHAN: I think we can certainly distinguish some trivial instances. I don't think the customary procedure of calling a judge "your honor," or his wearing dark robes, is law, but those written decisions embodying what we call a rule of law are in fact law. Just as I can say it is the law that you cannot break into a man's house at night and burglarize it, so there is a law that a judge must give a reason for his decision. Just as we would reverse the decision of a judge who did not convict a man for breaking into a house in the daytime with the intention of committing a felony because it wasn't a common-law crime of burglary, so we would reverse the decision of a judge who did not give reasons.

PAUL: Have the decisions of judges who didn't give reasons been reversed?

JONATHAN: Yes.

PAUL: Because of the fact that they did not give reasons for the decisions?

JONATHAN: Yes. But more than that, it's such an important principle that the decisions of an administrative body can also be reversed solely because it did not give reasons. According to administrative law, if a man had a reasonable administrative reason for making a decision, the rightness of his decision will not be questioned, but if he doesn't give a reason, it will. That's a simple way of putting it, and it applies in a more complex way to judges. They must give proper reasons or follow the rules governing trials.

PAUL: Are there any limits to the law? Does it cover every aspect of human existence, or does it stop with public acts?

JONATHAN: I'm not sure I understand what you mean.

PAUL: Does law intrude inside the family? What about a man's private life—how he spends his idle hours, what he reads in his home, with whom he speaks in his home, and so on? Has the law a right to come inside the home in this sense?

JONATHAN: It certainly has the right to come inside the home insofar as we recognize certain values to be at stake. We prosecute parents who beat their children so severely the kids are maimed. In such a case, the law says that the child is a ward of the state. The parent doesn't have an absolute right, and children are taken away from their parents quite often.

PAUL: Is there any limit to the law inside the home?

JONATHAN: Do you mean in practice or in theory?

PAUL: Both.

JONATHAN: The limits are practical ones. You can't know everything that goes on in a home, and people are certainly reluctant to investigate all private matters, but in theory the law does purport to regulate even the most intimate relationships of men and women. There are laws governing the sexual practices of married couples. In fact these laws are not enforced, so, as I said earlier, they are law in a lesser sense. Ideally, I think a law should enter only into private relations to prevent abuses against innocent or helpless people. I don't think you have a right to dictate sexual practices, but I do think you have a right to prevent parents from maiming children.

PAUL: I think we can now point up the difference between law, morality, and ethics. Suppose a man were to incur a debt. As I understand the law, there is a statute of limitations which means that after a given period of time, if he hasn't been asked to repay the debt, it is canceled. But morally the custom in that society might well be for men to pay the debts even of their parents, and ethically a man is surely indebted for whatever he borrowed, regardless of the statute of limitations. We owe the Waverly novels of Scott to the fact that Scott's partner disappeared with the funds, and that Scott, though he was legally free, decided that he was ethically obligated to raise the money.

JONATHAN: But the problem is more complicated: there is a doctrine of moral obligation in the law governing debts. If you promise to pay a debt after the statute of limitations has run out on that debt, your promise is enforceable.

PAUL: But suppose you don't make a subsequent promise?

JONATHAN: A debt is not as simple as you make it seem; it is a legal entity. You can owe money in various contexts for various reasons. For example, suppose you buy something that you're supposed to pay for, but the seller doesn't do anything to let you know he wants the money. Over the years you implicitly rely on the fact that he seems to have lost interest, and you begin to think of your purchase as a gift. Now, this diminution of obligation is what the law recognizes when it says a debt will not be enforceable after a certain time unless the debtor still believes he owes the money.

PAUL: I don't think this faces the issue.

JONATHAN: Let me put it to you in a simple way. If a man becomes legally bankrupt in this country, he extinguishes all his debts and can never be sued for them. Do you say that a man who has gone into bankruptcy has a moral obligation to pay those people whose debts have been extinguished?

PAUL: I think he might conceive of himself as having an ethical obligation; this has been the case a number of times in the past. I define a moral obligation as an obligation that people customarily assume. I don't think it's true today that most people feel morally bound to pay their debts after they've gone into bankruptcy. But a man can well conceive of himself as ethically bound, and in that sense the law and ethics are not altogether consonant.

JONATHAN: Perhaps I'm being too legalistic, but I do think a debt is a legal entity, not an ethical one.

PAUL: Let's talk about Walter Scott then.

JONATHAN: I can give you a better example than Walter Scott. I take it that you are arguing that a man could feel ethically obligated to pay off a family debt that the law didn't recognize. I would say that such a debt was achieved outside the law. It is without implicit reference to the law. For example, there is no statute of limitations or even rules for a gambling debt; the obligations involved exist outside the law. But a purchase made in the ordinary commercial world creates a debt that can be legally extinguished. What you're saying is that a debt can be something more than or other than a legal debt. I don't see that.

PAUL: But in a sense you said that too when you said that a gambling debt is made outside the law. Therefore, there is a world outside the law that can be governed by custom, by ethical ideals, by philosophical reflection, and by many other things. This shows that there are limits to the scope, applicability, and meaning of the law and that it cannot be used to define ethics or morality.

JONATHAN: I agree with everything you said except that last sentence. The fact that the law does not govern all possible relationships does not necessarily mean that it cannot or should not. In any case, I think it affects ethics and morality. I would say it should not govern all relations, but that doesn't mean it can't help redefine the meaning of morality and ideals in a particular society. I think, for example, that when we say that a man is obligated to pay taxes, we are in part defining what his obligation to his fellow man is.

PAUL: Is that also an ethical application of the law?

JONATHAN: Yes. I think that when a man is required by law to contribute money to the commonweal, his obligation is an ethical as well as a legal one.

PAUL: If I understand you correctly, implicit in what you are saying is a supposition of the sort made today by behaviorist psychologists. They say that anything that is knowable about a man is manifested in behavior, and that any discourse about minds, will, intention, and so on, not yet manifested in behavior, is meaningless. You say that whatever men do can in principle be brought under the aegis of the law. That may be the case, but that still does not mean that there are not areas which are defined in different ways and which ought to be recognized as operating under quite different principles than the law can possibly encompass.

JONATHAN: I think what you're saying may be correct but somewhat askew. There are certain operations—artistic acts, for example—on which the law can have little impact and in practice should have no impact. Legislating how much red can be used in a painting will not get to the essence of a painting. Since man is more than a behaving being, the law does not cover every aspect of him. Nevertheless, in the realm of human conduct we can legislate, although we may not affect the meaning of the conduct we are trying to regulate. We do, however, in principle have the ability to control the conditions and manifestations of that meaning in certain contexts.

PAUL: I agree with what you just said, but I'm still not clear about whether or not there is an intrinsic limit to the law. You argue that it would be wise for the law not to interfere with artists or with others in their privacy, but that in principle it could. I don't think it can. It can apply only to what is publicly manifest.

JONATHAN: We do deal with intentions in criminal law by a mode of inference from public actions, and therefore I suppose we could deal with the meaning of acts. We could pass a law limiting the use of red in paintings because we think red is a Communist color, but of course we should not, because the meaning of a painting is not a proper subject for law. We should try to regulate only conduct which is destructive or to encourage conduct which is conducive to a full life. We should not try to invade the realm where men are creative thinkers, even if we could perfect ways to control expressions of thought.

PAUL: I think now our difference is this: You speak as though in principle the law had absolute universal scope but wisdom dictates that it restrict itself, whereas I am suggesting that there are areas which the law cannot actually encompass and that the only intentions it can deal with are those derivable from overt acts.

JONATHAN: Right.

PAUL: The law cannot get to intentions that are never expressed in overt acts. It cannot get to the intent of an artist, no matter what he is in fact doing. It cannot get to the speculations of the philosopher if they are not written down. In this sense the law is limited to what is overt, to what is publicly exhibited.

JONATHAN: Fine. There are two separate points. One is what the law can proscribe; two, what the law can describe.

PAUL: Could I sharpen this by relating it to an issue with which you have done a great deal of illuminating work— the field of religion? A man who is religious has a relationship to God. This is a relationship to a being outside our space-time world. What the man says is one thing, but what he feels, what his attitude is, is another, distinguished in religion as the difference between the letter and the spirit. As far as I can see, the law can never get any further than the letter.

JONATHAN: Do you mean the letter of the law or the letter of religion?

PAUL: The letter of religion. People who perform rituals without much belief or with hatred in their hearts are not religious. They are merely going through a religious ritual. The law can say something about the performance of ritual, but it cannot make any judgment about the man in his privacy as he is alone with his God, or about his sincerity, his attitude, or his faith. These are outside and ought to be outside the realm of law.

JONATHAN: I am not sure how the religious example helps us. Let me get back to the difference between proscription and description. As far as description goes, I agree with you entirely. But insofar as I can treat man as a legal object and can have a mode of inference to intent which is somehow consistent and predictable, I can presumably have an effect on his mind. I can tell a painter he cannot paint with red. The law in principle can apply to all ranges of actions, though it cannot ultimately affect the private meaning of an act.

PAUL: It seems to me that you are now in a dilemma. On the one hand, you speak of the law as it is ideally, upholding its nobility and objectivity. On the other hand, you do not speak of the political situation as it is ideally, but instead speak of it as if it were always corrupt. Yet aren't the judges and the law part of the political system and therefore tainted in the same way as political leaders, policemen, and administrators are?

JONATHAN: I think that in fact they are tainted in the same way, but I don't think they are part of the political system.

PAUL: Then how would you distinguish the political world from the legal world?

JONATHAN: The political world is the world in which men decide how to govern themselves—what rules they want followed, what relationships they want controlled, etc. The legal world is a world in which these decisions are already given; it is the job of the legal world to see that the decision are carried out.

PAUL: Then the law in some sense is a set of norms and the political world a set of interplays of power?

JONATHAN: The law is a discipline in which particular results are arrived at by the application of certain principles. It is not a part of the political system, though it is set up to serve political ends. It is a profession and a body of rules.

PAUL: Do you not include the police, the sheriff, and other law-enforcement bodies as a part of the law?

JONATHAN: The problem with the police, the sheriff, and the law-enforcement bodies is that they aren't legal enough. They act arbitrarily in response to political pressures. Ideally a policeman should make an arrest only in accordance with a law. Right now many people argue that all the criminals are being let loose in the streets because the judges are coddling them. The fact is, it's not the judge's fault at all, for he follows the law; it's the policeman's fault. The police know very well when they hold somebody in illegal detention. They know when they beat him until he confesses. The police violate the law, and it is their fault if a guilty person is released, because it is their violation of the law that prevents a legal conviction.

PAUL: Now I think we have something very exciting. If I understand you correctly, you are suggesting that we have two distinct parties in our society. One is political and the other is legal. We apparently have quasi-legal political people such as policemen, sheriffs, and other law-enforcement officers. Your suggestion is that it would be preferable to make all law-enforcement bodies entirely subject to the legal structure?

JONATHAN: Absolutely.

PAUL: This is a rather unusual and arresting idea. What you're suggesting really is that the political organization create a body that would go its own way with its own kind of laws.

JONATHAN: That's precisely why we appoint judges for life tenure and why we expect them to follow the law in spite of their political background. But I want to return to the problem of the police. I hope it focuses the issue. If we let the police harass somebody for political reasons, or repeatedly prosecute somebody they know they cannot convict but want to punish politically, we violate the whole purpose of the law, which is to let people know what in fact they may do and what acts they are not criminally liable for.

PAUL: But one of the consequences of this very interesting idea is that the political and the legal systems can come into conflict.

JONATHAN: There is no question of that.

PAUL: Do you believe the political system should knuckle under wherever there is such a conflict?

JONATHAN: Yes, I think it should.

PAUL: But the political system has the power, and it will not necessarily knuckle under. We saw in Nazi Germany that just the reverse sometimes happens.

JONATHAN: That is not entirely true. Many Supreme Court decisions that declare laws unconstitutional cause a popular uproar, but the political system knuckles under because we all know that the job of the Supreme Court is to follow the law. And there is a choice. If you don't like the decision that the court hands down, you can alter the Constitution, or if it's not a constitutional matter, you can make a new law.

PAUL: If I understand you correctly, one of the consequences of your view would be that it would be wrong to engage in civil disobedience. Now isn't this a difficult conclusion for *you* to draw? In a previous chapter you stated that there were times when it was right for men to be civilly disobedient.

JONATHAN: But my point is that the political structure, having established the legal system, should accept its autonomy and submit to it. Now, what individuals who are not judges should do in terms of the law is an entirely different matter. There are times, I think, when you have to

recognize the fact that to have a political impact you
must violate the law.

PAUL: Oh, yes, I understand that, but I thought you said that
the political system should be subservient to the legal.

JONATHAN: Only insofar as it sets up the legal system to achieve its
ends and recognizes its importance as an autonomous
organ. But if we believe that the legal system is not
achieving its ends, we have a number of alternative ways
to handle the problem. The political system can change
the laws which the legal system must apply. An individual
can respond by violating both the law and the political
ideal of obeying the law. Sometimes when we are civilly
disobedient, we break both political and legal norms.

PAUL: Is such an action doubly wrong?

JONATHAN: No, because sometimes the only way to achieve what we
want as men is to go beyond law or even both politics and
law.

PAUL: I think perhaps this is a good place to end our discussion. At some later time we may want to consider whether
or not it is possible to have such a noble idea of the law
as you have expressed here and yet maintain some view
of civil disobedience.

Afterword

On this note—the relationship between civil disobedience and the autonomy and worth of law—we end this dialogue. By now some of the issues have been crystallized. Paul Weiss' basic perspective, repeatedly manifest throughout these pages, is that the state and the family, and eventually all mankind, have their own rationales in terms of which the achievements of individuals are to be understood, without compromising the fact that each individual has a dignity of his own, with rights and duties dictated by an ideal good. Jonathan Weiss conceives of mankind and nature as being more directly and intimately connected, each complementing and fulfilling the other. He attempts to explain the phenomena of obligation and responsibility as founded on common reliance to serve common goals and argues that moral decisions are made by weighing factors so as to be able to decide upon and implement the most amount of good.

This book exhibits an interplay of abstract ideas in the context of concrete problems. It is the hope of both father and son that some progress has been made in the understanding of the nature of man and of the world in which he lives, of obligations, responsibilities, and the rights of both the young and the old. Disagreements remain, particularly with respect to the fundamental grounds of morality and the way they determine the best modes of acting. A common core—the acknowledgment that sound moral judgments rest on more than individual preferences, that men are at once private individuals and beings to be understood in the context of society and the universe, and that there is promise in the pursuit of reasoned inquiry—lies behind all our divergencies. It establishes the possibility of further discussion by us and, it is hoped, by our readers.

Index

Index

land-grant colleges, 32
law, 176–201; "absolute natural,"
185; autonomy and worth of,
203–204; civil disobedience
and, 39–41, 113–114, 117–119,
201–203; common versus positive, 178; criminal, 191, 196;
custom and, 190–191; defined,
177; disobedience of in constitutional cases, 118; enforceable
and unenforceable, 188–189,
199; ethics and, 193–195; Jews
and, 184–185; judges and, 190–
191; limits of, 37, 193; morals
and, 187, 193; precedent and,
133–135, 191; religion and, 197;
treaties and, 189; unconstitutional, 118, 200
lawbreaking: citizen's obligation
to report, 18, 199; immorality
of, 37; self-understanding
through, 36
legal system, versus political,
200–201
legislation, law and, 196
leisure programs, 147–148
Leopold-Loeb case, 36
life: competitive nature of, 24;
values and, 158–159
Little, Lou, 23
Locke, John, 92
Lowell, Robert, 108–111
loyalty: family and, 66; hate
and, 130; to nation, 94–95; to
state, 90–91
loyalty oath, by college students,
31–34
lying, rules of, 22

MacArthur, Gen. Douglas, 97
Magna Charta, 134–135
Malcolm X, 118
man, universe and, 155–175; see
also individual
mankind, two meanings of, 121
Manpower Development Training Act, 141
marriage, family and, 50
Marx, Karl, 57
Marxism, 100–101
mass media, 124

mass murder, 133
Medicare, 107
Metaphysics (Aristotle), 177
Michelangelo Buonarotti, 124–
125
Michigan, University of, 24
military training, 32
misery, human, 140, 145
Molière, 124
monopolies, 102
Moslems, 98
moonlighting, 146
morality: authority and, 15;
ethics and, 187; private, 16
Mormons, 75–76, 188
mountain climbing, 28–31
movies, child's attendance at, 60–
61

nation, 89; loyalty to, 93–95;
"political," 95–96
national holidays, 96
natural law, 178–179, 182, 185
natural rights, 179
Nazis: legal system of, 182, 184;
in postwar Germany, 98; relationship with, 130–133
Negro: African background of,
153; civil rights for, 40, 142;
de facto segregation of, 150;
education for, 151; law and,
184; police and, 38; prejudice
against, 69–72; self-improve-
ment of, 152; special advantages for, 151–153; voter regis-
tration for, 113
New Masses, 148
New York, 90
New Zealand, 107
non-political action, 112–114
Nuremberg trials, 133–135

objectivity of truth assumed, 7
obligation, doctrine of, 4–45,
108–110, 154, 203–204
Oregon, 91

paideia, 30–31
Pakistan, 188
parent, permissive, 79

208